York Notes Rapid Revision
Romeo and Juliet

AQA GCSE English Literature

Written by Jo Heathcote

Pearson

YORK PRESS

The right of Jo Heathcote to be identified as the Author of this Work has been asserted by her in accordance with the Copyright, Designs and Patents Act 1988

YORK PRESS
322 Old Brompton Road, London SW5 9JH

PEARSON EDUCATION LIMITED
80 Strand, London, WC2R 0RL

© Librairie du Liban *Publishers* 2019

All rights reserved. No part of this publication may be reproduced, stored in a retrieval system, or transmitted in any form or by any means, electronic, mechanical, photocopying, recording, or otherwise, without either the prior written permission of the Publishers or a licence permitting restricted copying in the United Kingdom issued by the Copyright Licensing Agency Ltd, Barnard's Inn, 86 Fetter Lane, London EC4A 1EN

10 9 8 7 6 5 4 3 2 1

ISBN 978–1–2922–7090–6

Phototypeset by Carnegie Book Production
Printed in Slovakia

Photo credits:
J.Schelkle/Shutterstock for page 4 middle / gornostay/Shutterstock for page 6 bottom and page 30 middle / Mike H/Shutterstock for page 8 bottom / Erika Parfenova/© iStock for page 10 bottom, 14 bottom right and page 34 middle / Kiselev Andrey Valerevich/Shutterstock for page 12 middle and page 38 bottom / Paul Doyle/Alamy for page 12 bottom and page 42 top middle / Deborah Kolb/Shutterstock for page 14 bottom left and page 32 bottom / Elena.Katkova/Shutterstock for page 16 middle left, 40 middle and page 52 bottom / Ian Bottle/Alamy for page 16 middle right and page 40 bottom / Vince Reilly/Shutterstock for page 18 middle / Phovoir/Shutterstock for page 20 middle and page 38 middle / PAINTING/Alamy for page 24 top / The Picture Art Collection/Alamy for page 26 bottom / ermess/Shutterstock for page 28 middle / dny3d/Shutterstock for page 36 middle / Nomad_Soul/Shutterstock for page 42 bottom middle and page 50 bottom / valentinrussanov/© iStock for page 44 top / Yuri_Arcurs/© iStock for page 44 middle / Arturs Budkevics/Shutterstock for page 48 middle / joegolby/© iStock for page 54 top / lekcej/© iStock for page 58 middle / Niall_Majury/© iStock for page 60 middle

CONTENTS

PLOT AND STRUCTURE

Prologue and Act I Scene 1	4
Act I Scenes 2–5	6
Act II Scenes 1 and 2	8
Act II Scenes 3–6	10
Act III Scenes 1 and 2	12
Act III Scenes 3–5	14
Act IV	16
Act V	18
Form and structure	20
Quick revision	22

SETTING AND CONTEXT

Elizabethan society	24
Italian society	26
Settings	28
Quick revision	29

CHARACTERS

Romeo in Acts I and II	30
Romeo in Acts III–V	32
Juliet in Acts I and II	34
Juliet in Acts III–V	36
Mercutio and Tybalt	38
Lord and Lady Capulet	40
The Nurse and Friar Lawrence	42
Benvolio and Paris	44
Quick revision	46

THEMES

Love	48
Fate and free will	50
Family and marriage	52
Conflict and honour	54
Quick revision	56

LANGUAGE

Imagery and symbolism	58
Dramatic techniques	60

EXAM PRACTICE

Understanding the exam	62
Character questions	64
Planning your character response	66
Grade 5 annotated answer	68
Grade 7+ annotated answer	70
Theme questions	72
Planning your theme response	74
Grade 5 annotated answer	76
Grade 7+ annotated answer	78
Practice questions	80

GLOSSARY 82

ANSWERS 83

PLOT AND STRUCTURE Prologue and Act I Scene 1

Three key things about the Prologue and Act I Scene 1

1. The **Prologue** introduces **two rival families**: the **Capulets** and the **Montagues**.
2. It **foreshadows** the themes and events of the play.
3. We witness the **feud** between the two families, and are introduced to a **main character, Romeo**.

What happens in the Prologue?

- We are told of the lengthy disagreement between two old Verona families, the Capulets and the Montagues.
- We learn just how violent their quarrel has become.
- We are told that Montague and Capulet's own two children will fall in love and the quarrel will be ended only through their deaths.

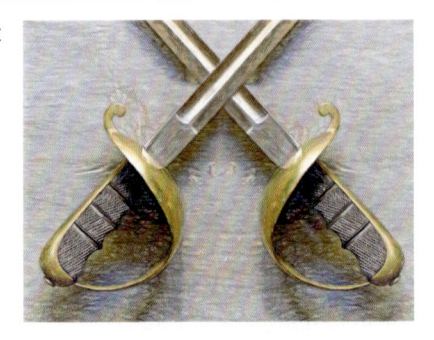

What happens in Scene 1?

- The servants of both households taunt each other in the street.
- We are introduced to Tybalt, a hot-blooded Capulet, and Benvolio, a peacekeeping Montague.
- A violent fight takes place on the street, stopped by the arrival of the Prince and the heads of both families.
- The Prince decrees there will be serious consequences if the violence continues.
- Lady Montague enquires where her son Romeo is as he was not involved in the fight.
- Benvolio finds Romeo, who seems sensitive and sad.
- Romeo confides in Benvolio that he is desperately in love with a Capulet called Rosaline, who does not return his love.
- Benvolio listens thoughtfully and gives Romeo sensible advice.

PLOT AND STRUCTURE Prologue and Act I Scene 1

Five key quotations

1. Dramatic technique of foreshadowing: **'From forth the fatal loins of these two foes/A pair of star-cross'd lovers take their life'** (Prologue.5–6)
2. Benvolio's good sense: **'Put up your swords, you know not what you do'** (I.1.59)
3. The theme of violence: **'What, drawn and talk of peace? I hate the word,/As I hate hell, all Montagues, and thee'** (Tybalt) (I.1.64–5)
4. Plot development: **'If ever you disturb our streets again,/Your lives shall pay the forfeit of the peace'** (The Prince) (I.1.90–1)
5. The language of opposites and oxymoron: **'O brawling love, O loving hate'** (Romeo) (I.1.170)

Note it!

Note how, despite the violence between the two families, Romeo is presented as sensitive and loving and Benvolio as sensible. Together, they provide a contrast to the hot-headed young men we see in the opening of the play and to Montague and Capulet themselves.

Exam focus

How can I write about character? AO1

You can explore some of Shakespeare's key messages by thinking about what certain characters represent.

Tybalt is shown to be hot-headed: he is quick to begin a fight, with his words 'Have at thee, coward.' He challenges Benvolio and is shown to be vicious. **Shakespeare provides a contrast** in Benvolio who tries to stop the fight and encourages Tybalt to **'Put up thy sword/Or manage it to part these men with me.'** In this way Shakespeare uses character to show us that two opposite forces are working against each other in the play right from the start.

- Describes Shakespeare's technique
- Quotation used to contrast the two characters
- Broader analysis of this use of character

Now you try!

Finish this paragraph about the character Benvolio. Use one of the quotations from the list above.

Shakespeare presents the character of Benvolio as sensible to contrast. ....

My progress Needs more work ☐ Getting there ☐ Sorted! ☐

5

PLOT AND STRUCTURE   Act I Scenes 2-5

Three key things about Act I Scenes 2-5

1. Juliet's father discusses her **future marriage** with Paris but at this point wants Juliet to **approve the match**. He holds a **feast** so they can meet.
2. The Montagues find out about the feast from a servant and **vow to attend** for some fun, though **Romeo is unhappy** at the idea.
3. **Juliet meets Romeo** at the feast for the first time and they are **immediately attracted** to each other. Only later do they discover they are from the **rival families**.

What happens in Scenes 2 and 3?

- Paris comes to Capulet to seek Juliet's hand in marriage. He feels his daughter is too young but will consent if she agrees.
- Capulet invites Paris to a feast he is holding and sends out a servant with invitations.
- Benvolio and Romeo meet the servant. He invites them to the feast not knowing they are Montagues.
- Juliet's mother talks to her about marriage and is keen she approves of Paris.
- We see how Juliet has a trusting relationship with her Nurse.

What happens in Scene 4?

- Benvolio and Romeo are joined by the other Montagues who are on their way to the Capulet feast with masks and torches. Romeo is still lovesick and has a bad feeling about them going.
- We meet lively Mercutio, Romeo's good friend. He paints a picture of love as a troubling fantasy planted in young minds by a fairy called Queen Mab.

What happens in Scene 5?

- The feast is busy and lively. Romeo sees Juliet for the first time.
- Tybalt notices Romeo and is immediately enraged that he is there.
- Romeo and Juliet meet and fall in love, discovering at the very end of the night they are from the feuding families.

PLOT AND STRUCTURE Act I Scenes 2-5

Five key quotations

1. The **theme** of marriage: **'Let two more summers wither in their pride,/ Ere we may think her ripe to be a bride'** (Capulet) (I.2.10–11)
2. The character of Lady Capulet: **'Tell me, daughter Juliet,/How stands your dispositions to be married?'** (I.3.65–6)
3. The theme of fate: **'Some consequence yet hanging in the stars/ Shall bitterly begin his fateful date/With this night's revels'** (Romeo) (I.4.107–9)
4. Romeo's character: **'Did my heart love till now? forswear it, sight!/ For I ne'er saw true beauty till this night'** (1.5.51–2)
5. An example of **foreshadowing**: **'If he be married,/My grave is like to be my wedding bed'** (Juliet) (I.5.133–4)

Note it!

Though the main focus of these scenes is love and marriage, Shakespeare draws attention to other actions and feelings. The party may be fun, but note how conflict and problems are foreshadowed through further evidence of Tybalt's fiery character. Note also Romeo and Juliet's anxiety about a possible future together given their backgrounds.

Exam focus

How can I write about a theme? AO1

You can use Act I to write about love and marriage, as many different viewpoints are explored here.

When Paris requests Juliet's hand in marriage, **Lord Capulet seems reluctant for Juliet to marry young as she is his only child.** He tells Paris to **'Let two more summers wither in their pride,/Ere we may think her ripe to be a bride.'** This suggests that Capulet is protective of his daughter who is 'the hopeful lady of my earth'. However, **later in the play his attitude changes and he forces Juliet into the marriage** when he thinks his authority as a father is being challenged.	Makes a point about one view of marriage Quotations used to illustrate the point Displays a wider knowledge of this theme across the play.

Now you try!

Finish this paragraph about how Lady Capulet views the proposal of marriage. Use one of the quotations from the list above.

Lady Capulet seems keen for Juliet to look positively at Paris and consider..................

My progress Needs more work ☐ Getting there ☐ Sorted! ☐

PLOT AND STRUCTURE Act II Scenes 1 and 2

Three key things about Act II Scenes 1 and 2

1. **Romeo** is in **love** but with **Juliet** now and **not Rosaline**.
2. He puts himself in **danger** by climbing into the **Capulet orchard** after the feast is over.
3. The two young lovers meet again, exchange **a vow of love** and decide to **marry without their parents' permission.**

What happens in Scene 1?

- Benvolio and Mercutio are out searching for Romeo after the feast.
- We learn that Benvolio is concerned for his friend, whilst Mercutio mocks his lovesick nature. They do not realise he is with Juliet.

What happens in Scene 2?

- Romeo climbs the wall into the Capulet orchard and sees Juliet at her window.
- He overhears her talking about her feelings for him and calls to her.
- Juliet is embarrassed at being overheard, but concerned her family will find him there and his life will be in danger.
- Romeo declares his feelings of love for Juliet.
- Juliet in turn declares her love.
- Juliet asks Romeo to arrange for them to be married if his feelings towards her are true.

PLOT AND STRUCTURE Act II Scenes 1 and 2

Five key quotations

1. The use of **imagery**: **'It is the east, and Juliet is the sun.'** (Romeo) (II.2.3)
2. The meaning of the family feud: **'Tis but thy name that is my enemy;/ Thou art thyself, though not a Montague.'** (Juliet) (II.2.38–9)
3. The **theme** of love: **'With love's light wings did I o'erperch these walls,/For stony limits cannot hold love out'** (Romeo) (II.2.66–7)
4. The use of **foreshadowing**: **'It is too rash, too unadvis'd, too sudden'** (Juliet) (II.2.118)
5. The theme of marriage: **'If that thy bent of love honourable,/Thy purpose marriage, send me word tomorrow'** (Juliet) (II.2.143–4)

Note it!

Note how aware Juliet is of the danger they are both in. She worries that if Romeo is found in the orchard, the Capulets may kill him. Although she seems more wary and thoughtful than the impetuous Romeo, it is Juliet who asks him to arrange their marriage for the very next day.

Exam focus

How can I write about language? AO2

You can use Scene 2 to write about imagery connected with light and the heavens.

Romeo describes Juliet using **metaphors** of light, saying **'It is the east, and Juliet is the sun'**, and describing her as a **'bright angel'** and a **'winged messenger'**. The effect is that Romeo sees Juliet as heavenly and beautiful. She seems to represent all that is good, innocent and bright to him, but the metaphor as he gazes up at her also suggests he sees her as a type of goddess.

- Language technique used by Shakespeare
- Selected textual details as examples
- Thoughtful comment on the effect of the metaphor
- Develops the idea

Now you try!

Finish this paragraph about imagery. Use one of the quotations from the list above.

Romeo also describes his love for Juliet as giving him wings ....

My progress — Needs more work ☐   Getting there ☐   Sorted! ☐

PLOT AND STRUCTURE   Act II Scenes 3-6

Three key things about Act II Scenes 3-6

1. The **Nurse and Friar Lawrence** become involved in Romeo and Juliet's **secret love plot**.
2. **Romeo** reassures the **Nurse** of his **genuine love and commitment** whilst **Juliet waits anxiously** for news.
3. The **lovers meet** at **Friar Lawrence's cell** to be **married**.

What happens in Scene 3?

- We meet Friar Lawrence and see Romeo ask him to perform the wedding ceremony.
- The Friar is concerned at how quickly Romeo has decided to marry Juliet but feels the marriage may help to end the two families' feud.

What happens in Scene 4?

- Benvolio learns that Tybalt has sent a challenge to Romeo's house.
- Romeo arrives but is intercepted by the Nurse who is waiting to take news to Juliet.
- Romeo asks the Nurse to make sure Juliet can come that afternoon to Friar Lawrence's cell to be married.

What happens in Scenes 5 and 6?

- Juliet waits impatiently for the Nurse to return with news.
- The Nurse returns and tells Juliet Romeo has kept his promise.
- Romeo and the Friar await Juliet's arrival at the cell.
- When Juliet arrives, the lovers greet each other with a kiss.
- The Friar leads the young couple away to be married.

PLOT AND STRUCTURE Act II Scenes 3–6

Five key quotations

1. Romeo reveals his plan: **'my heart's dear love is set/On the fair daughter of rich Capulet'** (II.3.57–8)
2. Friar Lawrence's hope: **'For this alliance may so happy prove/To turn your households' rancour to pure love'** (II.3.90–2)
3. The Nurse's comic warning: **'if ye should lead her in a fool's paradise, as they say, it were a very gross kind of behaviour'** (II.4.151–2)
4. Romeo keeps his promise: **'And there she shall at Friar Lawrence' cell/Be shriv'd and married'** (II.4.163–6)
5. The theme of fate: **'These violent delights have violent ends'** (Friar Lawrence) (II.6.9)

Note it!
Although the couple are about to marry, which we might associate with love and happiness, note there are many references to death, sorrow and violence, suggesting the tragedy to come.

Exam focus

How can I write about character? AO1

You can write about the Nurse's character and actions to consider whether Romeo and Juliet were right to seek her help.

> The Nurse reveals that she has been employed to take care of Juliet since she was a baby. **She seems genuinely concerned that Juliet does not make a mistake in marrying Romeo** and reminds him that, **'if ye should lead her in a fool's paradise, as they say, it were a very gross kind of behaviour'**. However, she goes ahead and helps Juliet to marry Romeo secretly knowing that Capulet is arranging a marriage with Paris. **In this way, she could be said to be irresponsible in her care of Juliet.**

- Clear point showing character's role
- Key quotation for theme
- Considers another interpretation

Now you try!

Finish this paragraph about the Friar and his actions at this point. Use one of the quotations from the list above.

The Friar also seems genuinely concerned about Romeo...

My progress   Needs more work ☐   Getting there ☐   Sorted! ☐

PLOT AND STRUCTURE   Act III Scenes 1 and 2

Three key things about Act III Scenes 1 and 2

1. There is a **swift change** of atmosphere as a **violent fight** erupts between the Capulets and Montagues.
2. Both Mercutio and Tybalt **lose their lives** in the fight.
3. By contrast, **Juliet waits** for Romeo on their **wedding night**.

What happens in Scene 1?

- It is a hot afternoon and Benvolio is anxious to keep the Montagues out of trouble.
- Tybalt arrives. He is looking for Romeo to whom he has issued a challenge, as he was insulted by Romeo's attendance at the feast.
- Romeo tries to keep the peace. Tybalt and the Montagues are unaware he has just married Juliet – a Capulet.
- Mercutio cannot understand why Romeo does not rise to the challenge so he fights Tybalt himself.
- Mercutio is stabbed as Romeo tries to break them apart. Mercutio dies from his wound.
- Enraged, Romeo chases after Tybalt to avenge his friend. Tybalt is injured and dies. Romeo flees the scene.
- The Prince arrives and banishes Romeo from Verona for his actions.

What happens in Scene 2?

- Juliet is waiting for night to fall so that Romeo can visit her in secret.
- The Nurse returns and is very upset, bringing the news of Tybalt's death.
- She reveals that Romeo has been banished from Verona for killing Tybalt.
- Juliet is distraught at the news, both of Tybalt's death and that her husband is to be banished.
- The Nurse promises to find Romeo and bring him to her.

PLOT AND STRUCTURE Act III Scenes

Five key quotations

1. Romeo as peacemaker: **'I do protest I never injured thee,/But love thee better than thou canst devise'** (III.1.65–6)
2. The theme of violent conflict: **'A plague a'both your houses!'** (Mercutio) (III.1.102)
3. The theme of fate: **'O, I am fortune's fool'** (III.1.132)
4. The outcome of the fight: **'Tybalt is gone and Romeo banished,/Romeo that kill'd him, he is banished.'** (Nurse) (III.2.69–70)
5. The theme of family honour: **'Will you speak well of him that kill'd your cousin?** (Nurse) /**'Shall I speak ill of him that is my husband?'** (Juliet) (III.2.96–7)

Note it!
Note how Shakespeare uses **contrast**, for example by **juxtaposing** the marriage of Romeo and Juliet in Act II with the violent fight scene in Act III. Consider how these contrasts echo the conflicting emotions we see in the play.

Exam focus

How can I write about plot? AO1
You can explore how events turn against Romeo from this point and threaten the future of the newly married couple.

> Romeo is drawn into the fight against his will. **He pleads with Tybalt not to fight but does not make it plain he has married Juliet**, instead telling him, **'I never injured thee,/But love thee better than thou canst devise'**. In this way, **the secret marriage to Juliet cannot help to stop the feud and the indirectness of Romeo's words only confuses and angers both Tybalt and Mercutio.**

- A clear point about the plot
- Quotation used to support the point
- Analyses the impact of the action

Now you try!
Finish this paragraph about the impact of the fight. Use one of the quotations from the list above.

We see the impact of the fight when Mercutio ....

My progress — Needs more work ☐ Getting there ☐ Sorted! ☐

STRUCTURE Act III Scenes 3–5

Key things about Act III Scenes 3–5

1. The **Friar** organises **a rescue plan** for the two lovers, worried that **Romeo** may choose to **take his own life**.
2. **Capulet** makes **a sudden decision** that his daughter should **marry Paris**.
3. **Romeo and Juliet say farewell** after spending just **one night** together.

What happens in Scene 3?

- Romeo turns to the Friar who gives him the news of his banishment.
- Romeo sees the punishment as worse than death and threatens to take his own life.
- The Nurse interrupts them with news of Juliet's distress.
- They arrange for Romeo to spend the wedding night with Juliet.
- The Friar reassures Romeo that all will be well but tells him he must go to Mantua the next morning and await news.

What happens in Scene 4?

- Lord and Lady Capulet discuss Juliet's grief – believing it to be for Tybalt.
- Capulet decides to arrange her marriage to Paris as soon as possible.
- Lady Capulet is to inform Juliet that the wedding will be in three days' time.

What happens in Scene 5?

- Romeo and Juliet wake in the early morning but realise they must part.
- The Nurse warns the lovers that Lady Capulet is on her way to see Juliet.
- The lovers part hastily.
- Lady Capulet tells Juliet she will wed Paris.
- Juliet is devastated and refuses to cooperate.
- Capulet arrives and is angry with Juliet.
- Juliet seeks comfort from the Nurse who advises her to forget Romeo and marry Paris.
- Juliet arranges to see the Friar under the pretence of going to confession.

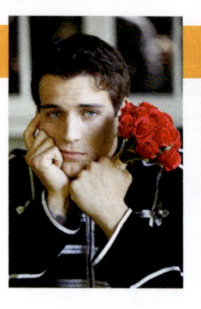

PLOT AND STRUCTURE Act III Scenes 3-5

Five key quotations

1. Romeo's reaction to his punishment: **'There is no world without Verona walls'** (III.3.17–18)
2. A father's authority in arranging a marriage: **'I think she will be rul'd/In all respects by me;'** (Capulet) (III.4.13–14)
3. The theme of fate: **'I have an ill-divining soul!/Methinks I see thee now, thou art so low,/As one dead in the bottom of a tomb'** (Juliet) (III.5.54–6)
4. Capulet's anger: **'disobedient wretch!/I tell thee what: get thee to church a'Thursday,/Or never after look me in the face'** (III.5.160–2)
5. Lady Capulet accepts Capulet's decision: **'Talk not to me, for I'll not speak a word./Do as thou wilt, for I have done with thee.'** (III.5.202–3)

Note it!

Note how the Nurse changes her advice to Juliet. After being her trusted helper, once she witnesses Capulet's angry display of power, she immediately advises Juliet to forget Romeo.

Exam focus

How can I write about context? AO3

You can use ideas about Capulet's decision to comment on the social context of the play.

> Though Capulet said Juliet should agree before marrying Paris in Act I, the violent events make him reconsider his plans for Juliet. Perhaps he fears Paris will no longer wish to be associated with the family and so uses his authority over Juliet to enforce the marriage. He asserts that she 'will be rul'd/In all respects by me', showing how he can take this decision as Juliet's father. Lady Capulet accepts this and follows her husband's orders, revealing how male authority was absolute over women at the time.

- Makes a clear statement establishing the plot
- Offers an interpretation of Capulet's actions
- Quotation used to support the point
- Analyses how the context can link to meaning

Now you try!

Finish this paragraph about how the response of Juliet's mother reflects the social context of the time. Use one of the quotations from the list above.

Juliet's mother reacts by ....

My progress   Needs more work ☐   Getting there ☐   Sorted! ☐

15

PLOT AND STRUCTURE Act IV

Three key things about Act IV

1. The Friar proposes an **elaborate plan**: Juliet will **fake her own death** to avoid marriage to Paris and be **reunited** with Romeo.
2. Juliet **deceives her parents** and the Nurse by **seemingly agreeing** to the wedding.
3. Juliet is found, **apparently dead**, on the wedding morning.

What happens in Scene 1?

- Paris asks the Friar's advice about his marriage to Juliet.
- Juliet arrives and evades Paris's questions about her feelings for him.
- Paris leaves, and Juliet shows the Friar how desperate she is by threatening to take her own life.
- The Friar tells Juliet of a potion to fake her own death.
- He suggests a plan whereby he and Romeo would be at the Capulet tomb when she wakes. The lovers could escape to Mantua.

What happens in Scenes 2 and 3?

- The Capulets are organising the wedding.
- Capulet is delighted when Juliet returns from the Friar, agreeing to the marriage.
- The marriage is brought forward to Wednesday.
- On the eve of her wedding Juliet asks the Nurse and her mother to leave her. She speaks of her fears about the Friar's plan and of waking in the tomb alone.
- She drinks the potion and falls unconscious.

What happens in Scenes 4 and 5?

- It is early morning on the wedding day and the Capulets are still preparing.
- The Nurse discovers Juliet's 'dead' body.
- Lord and Lady Capulet are overcome with grief.
- Paris and the Friar arrive and the wedding day becomes a funeral.

PLOT AND STRUCTURE   Act IV

Five key quotations

1. Juliet's strength of feeling: **'O bid me leap, rather than marry Paris,/ From off the battlements of any tower'** (IV.1.77–8)
2. The Friar's plan: **'Take thou this vial, being then in bed,/And this distilling liquor drink thou off'** (IV.1.93–4)
3. Juliet pretends to be obedient: **'Pardon, I beseech you!/Henceforward I am ever rul'd by you'** (IV.2.21–2)
4. Dramatic tension in Juliet's questioning: **'What if this mixture do not work at all?/Shall I be married then tomorrow morning?'** (IV.3.21–2)
5. The theme of fate: **'The heavens do low'r upon you for some ill;/Move them no more by crossing their high will'** (IV.5.94–5)

Note it!
Note that in Act IV the Friar continues to keep Romeo and Juliet's secret even when the situation has become serious. Remember that he has married the couple in secret and 'acted' when Juliet's 'dead' body is found. Perhaps he fears punishment for his role in the plot.

Exam focus

How can I write about language? AO2
You can use ideas from Juliet's soliloquy to comment on her thoughts and feelings.

Juliet is shown to be fearful and anxious about the Friar's plan. We see this in her soliloquy when she questions, 'What if this mixture do not work at all? Shall I be married then tomorrow morning?' From her speech we can see how isolated Juliet is – she no longer has anyone to confide in and must act alone. There is a sense of panic in her questions yet she bravely goes through with the plan.

- Topic sentence about Juliet's feelings
- Quotation used to support the point
- Interprets the feelings in relation to the plot
- Develops idea of how language conveys emotions

Now you try!
Finish this paragraph about a different feeling Juliet experiences elsewhere in Act IV. Use one of the quotations from the list above.

Juliet is also presented as quite capable of deception when ....

My progress   Needs more work ☐   Getting there ☐   Sorted! ☐

PLOT AND STRUCTURE Act V

Three key things about Act V

1. **Romeo** learns of **Juliet's death** before the **Friar's letter** arrives.
2. **Friar Lawrence**'s plan begins to **fall apart**.
3. **Romeo** and **Juliet take their own lives** in a final **cruel twist of fate**.

What happens in Scene 1?

- Balthasar has hurried to Mantua to give Romeo the news of Juliet's death.
- Romeo immediately sets off for Verona.
- He stops only to collect a deadly poison from a poor apothecary, planning to use this to take his own life if he finds Juliet is dead.

What happens in Scene 2?

- Friar John returns Friar Lawrence's letter having been unable to deliver it to Romeo.
- Friar Lawrence is driven to panic and rethinks his plan.

What happens in Scene 3?

- Paris visits Juliet's body at the tomb where he is met by Romeo.
- Paris and Romeo fight and Paris is killed.
- Believing Juliet to be dead, Romeo swallows the poison.
- Friar Lawrence arrives and meets Balthasar, learning Romeo is in the tomb.
- Juliet begins to wake and, seeing Romeo dead, refuses to leave with the Friar, who flees in fear.
- Juliet uses Romeo's dagger to take her own life.
- The Friar is captured by watchmen and, with Balthasar, tells the Prince of the secret marriage.
- The Montagues and the Capulets are reconciled in their shared grief.

PLOT AND STRUCTURE Act V

Five key quotations

1. The theme of fate: **'I defy you, stars!'** (Romeo) (V.1.24)
2. The themes of love and death: **'Arms, take your last embrace! and, lips, O you/The doors of breath, seal with a righteous kiss'** (Romeo) (V.3.112–14)
3. Use of oxymoron: **'O happy dagger,/This is thy sheath; there rust and let me die'** (Juliet) (V.3.169–70)
4. The Friar's story: **'Romeo, there dead, was husband to that Juliet,/And she, there dead, that Romeo's faithful wife.'** (V.3.231–2)
5. The structure comes full circle: **'Where be these enemies? Capulet, Montague?/See what a scourge is laid upon your hate'** (the Prince) (V.3.291–3)

Note it!

Note how Paris is presented as honourable throughout the play. His courtship follows the conventions of Veronese society and he is genuinely affected by Juliet's death, laying flowers in her tomb. Consider whether Capulet's choice for Juliet could have been a wise one in retrospect.

Exam focus

How can I write about a theme? (AO1)

You can write about how the final Act explores whether fate has played a part in the tragedy.

Throughout the play there are many references to fate, chance or the work of the stars being responsible for what happens to Romeo and Juliet. At the end of the play even the Prince feels 'That heaven finds means to kill your joys with love!' However, it could be argued that from the turning point of Mercutio's death to the Friar's letter being undelivered, we see how the human chain of events and miscommunication may have caused the deaths of Romeo and Juliet.

- Topic sentence makes overall point
- Quotation used to support the point
- Develops a different interpretation

Now you try!

Finish this paragraph about the use of chance, fate or the stars. Use one of the quotations from the list above.

Romeo reacts strongly when he hears that Juliet ....

My progress Needs more work ☐   Getting there ☐   Sorted! ☐

PLOT AND STRUCTURE Form and structure

Three key things about form and structure

1. *Romeo and Juliet* is a play made up of **five Acts**.
2. The play borrows some elements of a **classical tragedy** by centring on **high-status families**, themes of **loss and death** and **fast-paced action**.
3. The **time span** of the play is crucial to the action, covering only a **few days** from the **feast** on the **Sunday** to the **death** of the lovers on **Thursday** evening.

Why is the play structured into five Acts?

The structure of Shakespeare's play in five Acts is based on classical structures for drama, most closely associated with the Ancient Greeks and Romans. It is made up of:

1. **Exposition** (an initial incident): the fight in Act I
2. **Rising action** (a growth in tension): the meeting of the two lovers and their secret wedding
3. **Climax** (the high point of the action): the deaths of Mercutio and Tybalt
4. **Falling action** (where the plot unravels): Juliet's desperate situation in taking the potion
5. **Denouement** (the resolution): the deaths of the two lovers and the reconciliation of their families

What is blank verse?

- **Blank verse** is a type of poetry that does not rhyme, but which has a clear pattern of ten syllables in each line.
- This creates a rhythm in Shakespeare's **dialogue**.

Why does Shakespeare use so much contrast and opposition in the play?

- Shakespeare **juxtaposes** moments of high drama and hectic action with quieter, more reflective scenes. For example, Capulet's noisy and hectic feast in Act I Scene 5 is followed by the love scene in Capulet's orchard in Act II Scene 1.
- This structure heightens the tension and makes a dramatic contrast. It emphasises how the sequence of events leads the two young lovers to their tragic ending.

PLOT AND STRUCTURE Form and structure

Five key quotations

1. Setting the scene: **'The fearful passage of their death-mark'd love ... Is now the two hours' traffic of our stage'** (Prologue. 9–12)
2. Reflecting on the past: **'Who set this ancient quarrel new abroach?'** (Montague) (I.1.98)
3. Fast pace of the relationship: **'It is too rash, too unadvis'd, too sudden,/Too like the lightning.'** (Juliet) (II.2.118–20)
4. Impact of the speedily arranged marriage: **'Monday, ha, ha! Well, Wednesday is too soon,/ A'Thursday let it be—a'Thursday, tell her'** (Capulet) (III.4.19–20)
5. The Friar's timely warning: **'Wisely and slow, they stumble that run fast'** (II.3.94)

Note it!

Shakespeare uses subtle twists in the **plot** to maintain tension. Think about how he constructs a way to ensure the Montagues are at the feast; how he ensures it is Romeo who kills Tybalt; the way the Friar is unable to reach Romeo with the message before Balthasar arrives.

Exam focus

How can I write about pace and time? (AO2)

Despite a number of tender moments, the action of the play moves fast. You can use this to comment on the structure of the drama.

> Shakespeare uses characters such as Friar Lawrence to indicate the swift pace with which the lovers meet, fall in love and marry. He advises, 'Wisely and slow. They stumble that run fast.' His warnings reflect the rapid manner in which Romeo's infatuation with Rosaline has transformed into love for Juliet. Shakespeare seems to show us that youth can make us act hastily and perhaps without thought.

- Comment on a structural feature
- Supporting quotation for the point
- Inference about how pace is used
- Develops point to show dramatic purpose

Now you try!

Finish this paragraph to show a character behaving hastily. Use one of the quotations from the list above.

However, Shakespeare also shows us that it is not just the young who ....

My progress Needs more work ☐   Getting there ☐   Sorted! ☐

PLOT AND STRUCTURE Quick revision

1. Look at the calendar below. Work back through the play and collect as many quotations as you can that refer to time. Identify who makes the reference. Some examples have been given.
2. When you have found as many as you can:
   a) decide in which Act the passing of time is most important
   b) identify which character or characters are most anxious about the passing of time.

Sunday	Romeo: 'Is the day so young?'
Monday	Friar Lawrence: 'The grey ey'd morn smiles on the frowning night'
Tuesday	
Wednesday	
Thursday	The Prince: 'A glooming peace this morning with it brings'

Quick quiz

Answer these quick questions about the play's plot and structure.
1. Who tries to stop the fighting in Act I Scene 1?
2. Who is Romeo infatuated with at the start of the play?
3. Who visits Capulet to ask for his daughter's hand in marriage?
4. How do the Montagues find out about the Capulet feast?
5. Who asks Juliet, 'How stands your dispositions to be married?'?

PLOT AND STRUCTURE Quick revision

6. Which member of the Capulet household recognises Romeo's voice at the feast?
7. When Romeo sees Juliet at her window, what does he compare her to?
8. What does Juliet promise to do the next morning?
9. Where should Juliet go to for the secret wedding?
10. Who has been waiting since 'The clock struck nine'?
11. Why does Benvolio suggest to Mercutio they should go indoors in Act III Scene 1?
12. Who calls Tybalt a 'rat-catcher'?
13. What curse does Mercutio make as he dies from his wounds?
14. What item of jewellery does Juliet send with the Nurse when she goes to find Romeo?
15. What day does Capulet initially plan the wedding for?
16. Which city is Romeo to travel to when he leaves Juliet?
17. Who does Juliet meet at Friar Lawrence's cell when she goes for advice?
18. Name two things Juliet is frightened of as she is about to take the potion.
19. Who fails to deliver Friar Lawrence's letter?
20. Who does Romeo fight outside the Capulet vault?

Power paragraphs

Write a paragraph in response to **each of these questions**. For each, try to **use one quotation** you have learned from this section.

1. Why is Mercutio's death important to the plot?
2. In what ways is Friar Lawrence helpful or unhelpful to the young lovers?

Exam practice

Re-read Juliet's speech at the beginning of Act III Scene 2.

What does this speech show about Juliet and her actions, thoughts and feelings? Write **two paragraphs** explaining your ideas. You could comment on:

- Juliet's impatience for the night and why she is waiting for Romeo
- how she compares Romeo to the heavens.

My progress   Needs more work   Getting there   Sorted!

SETTING AND CONTEXT Elizabethan society

Five key things about Elizabethan life and society

1. The **Elizabethan period** describes the time when **Queen Elizabeth I** was on the throne.
2. The **timespan** of the period is from **1558 to 1603**.
3. Society was seen as a **very strict hierarchy** with the **Queen** at the **very top**.
4. It was a time of **exploration and discovery**, when famous explorers such as **Francis Drake** and **Walter Raleigh** set out to seek new lands or the 'new world'.
5. This period is known as the Renaissance, which is French for 'rebirth'. It was a time of **great learning** with huge developments in producing **works of art, poetry and plays**.

What was happening at the royal court and in the world of theatre?

- The English renaissance led to a flourishing world of theatre and plays. Young men such as William Shakespeare, Ben Jonson and Christopher Marlowe benefited from an education in their home towns and brought their writing talents to London.
- The court was the household that surrounded Queen Elizabeth. Some playwrights, including Shakespeare, were invited to perform their works here.
- Many playhouses existed in London with their companies of actors performing for the city's huge population. Theatres were very popular and lively with the audience moving around, gossiping and eating refreshments.
- Acting companies were all male at the time, with female characters being played by boys. Acting by women was frowned upon.

Why were people's beliefs and superstitions important?

- Many people believed that the monarch was appointed by God, as his representative on Earth. Attending church every Sunday was compulsory and there was a strong belief in Heaven and Hell.
- Fear of witchcraft and magic was common in Elizabethan England. Any 'unnatural' event caused suspicion as people struggled to find rational explanations.

SETTING AND CONTEXT Elizabethan society

Three key quotations

1. Religious imagery: **'Good pilgrim, you do wrong your hand too much … And palm to palm is holy palmers' kiss'** (Juliet) (I.5.96–9)
2. The power of Nature for good and evil: **'Within the infant rind of this weak flower/Poison hath residence, and medicine power'** (Friar Lawrence) (II.3.23–4)
3. Fear of the supernatural in the crypt: **'methinks I see my cousin's ghost/Seeking out Romeo that did spit his body/Upon a rapier's point. Stay, Tybalt, stay!'** (Juliet) (IV.4.55–7)

Note it!

From the Prologue onwards, note how many times fate is mentioned or referred to in the play. Romeo and Juliet are both superstitious and have a real sense that what they are doing will lead to disastrous consequences.

Exam focus

How do I link context to a response? AO2 AO3

Rather than using historical facts in a blunt way, write about context more subtly to aid your discussion of key themes such as superstition.

Shakespeare uses different kinds of opposition in the play to show natural forces pulling against what is unnatural.	Opening statement linked to a key theme
Friar Lawrence, for example uses images of the natural world which host potential evil, 'Within the infant rind of this weak flower/Poison hath residence, and medicine power'.	Supporting quotation
This reminds us that while the natural love between Romeo and Juliet has the potential to resolve the feud and bring order, their 'unnatural' deception leads to their downfall.	Explores the idea and links to the play's wider context
Perhaps this represents a moral message to Shakespeare's audience about going against the natural order.	Suggests a key underlying message

Now you try!

Finish this paragraph linking context to ideas about the supernatural. Use one of the quotations from the list above.

Shakespeare shows us how fearful Juliet is of the crypt, suggesting ....

My progress Needs more work ☐ Getting there ☐ Sorted! ☐

SETTING AND CONTEXT Italian society

Five key things about Renaissance Italy and its society

1. During the **Renaissance**, Italy was not one country but a whole **collection of city states** ruled by **powerful leaders**, such as the Prince in the play.
2. Bordered on three sides by the **Mediterranean** it benefited from the growth in **trade and exploration** at this time.
3. **Verona** was one of the states where **powerful and high-status, wealthy families** lived.
4. Sometimes the states **fought** against each other for **land and power**.
5. **Catholicism** was the **main religion**.

What was Italy like in Shakespeare's time?

- Italy grew wealthy through trade and became a centre for art, fashion, textiles, painting, literature, sculpture and music.
- Many famous artists and sculptors flourished under the patronage of rich Italian families. An artist would be paid well to complete an important piece of work for a family.
- Italian folktales, culture and politics were the inspiration for many of Shakespeare's plays, including *Romeo and Juliet*.

What is a patriarchal society and how did it affect marriage?

- A patriarchal society is one that is male-dominated. It springs from the idea that God is represented as male and has absolute power in the universe.
- In a family, the father had absolute power over the household and held all of the wealth and land. Women were rarely able to inherit their family wealth.
- As a result of this patriarchy, a father had the right to arrange his daughter's marriage, often to extend the power and influence of the family.
- Such a marriage would involve the payment of a dowry to the future husband – a gift of property or money. If a family did not have enough money to pay a dowry for all of its daughters, the remaining ones would go into a convent to live a spiritual life.

SETTING AND CONTEXT Italian society

Three key quotations

1. Conflict between families: 'Two households, both alike in dignity,/In fair Verona (where we lay our scene),/From ancient grudge break to new mutiny' (Prologue.1–3)
2. Arranged marriage: 'Now by Saint Peter's Church and Peter too,/He shall not make me there a joyful bride.' (Juliet) (III.5.116–17)
3. Patriarchy: 'And you be mine, I'll give you to my friend;/And you be not, hang, beg, starve, die in the streets' (Capulet) (III.5.191–2)

Note it!

Note how Lady Capulet sees nothing unusual in Juliet's swiftly arranged marriage. It implies she too may have had no choice in her marriage partner. For a young woman of high status, it was important to secure her family's wealth by marrying into money herself.

Exam focus

How do I link context to the themes of the play? AO3

Aim to weave context points about society into your responses rather than adding them at the start or end of your answer.

> Juliet responds with anger and fear to the news of her marriage. We sense her panic and anxiety when she exclaims, 'He shall not make me there a joyful bride'. Shakespeare shows us how powerfully a father could control his daughter's future and how Juliet has taken away this power by marrying Romeo without permission. She now also faces a spiritual dilemma in that she was married by the Friar in a religious ceremony and cannot marry again.

- Links to character's feelings and response makes overall point
- Supporting quotation
- Comments on social context
- Explores religious content

Now you try!

Write a paragraph in which you explore Capulet's position and response to Juliet's resistance. Use one of the quotations from the list above.

Capulet shows his power when he ....

My progress   Needs more work ☐   Getting there ☐   Sorted! ☐

SETTING AND CONTEXT Settings

Five key things about setting in the play

1. The play is set in the **wealthy city-state** of **Verona**.
2. Much of the **violent action** between the **feuding families** takes place in the **city streets**.
3. **Capulet's house** is the **central location** and is the place where **Juliet** meets her **'ill-starr'd' love**.
4. **Friar Lawrence's cell** is the place where both **Romeo** and **Juliet** turn for **advice** and where they are **secretly married**.
5. The **ending of the play** takes place at the **Capulet tomb (or vault)**, which houses the **family's dead** and becomes the scene of the **final tragic outcome**.

How do the streets of Verona add to the drama?

- The streets are the place where the hot-headed young men of both families spend their time and provoke each other.
- They are the site where **'three civil brawls'** have disturbed the peace and tested the patience of the Prince.
- On a hot day, Verona's streets provide the backdrop to the fight that makes **'worms' meat'** of Mercutio and kills Tybalt.

Why is Capulet's house significant?

- Capulet's house is where Paris comes to seek Juliet's hand in marriage.
- Capulet opens up his house for the feast and unwittingly invites the Montagues. In this sense, he paves the way for Romeo to meet his daughter in her own house.
- It is in Capulet's orchard that Romeo sees Juliet at her window. Shakespeare's use of contrast makes this beautiful setting a place of danger, and Juliet warns Romeo, **'The orchard walls are high and hard to climb,/ And the place death, considering who thou art,/If any of my kinsmen find thee here.'**

SETTING AND CO...

What do the scenes at Friar Lawrence's cell add?

- Initially Friar Lawrence's cell provides a peaceful location where Romeo comes for help and support. Romeo and Juliet come here to be secretly married.
- This changes after Act III Scene 1. Romeo rushes to the cell for aid and threatens to take his life. Juliet rushes here in distress when she learns she is to be married to Paris. The place of calm becomes the place of panic.

Is the final setting symbolic?

- The Capulet tomb becomes the supernatural setting that Juliet imagines before she takes the potion.
- To Romeo, Juliet's beauty **'makes/This vault a feasting presence full of light'**. A cruel irony means he does not realise she is still alive.
- Juliet's imaginings are eclipsed by the real horror of the two families discovering their young heirs and **'the hopeful lady of my earth'** dead in the tomb.

Quick quiz

1. What was interesting about the acting companies in Shakespeare's time?
2. Name one example of a character believing in superstition.
3. Which country provided much inspiration for Shakespeare?
4. Name one character whose dialogue uses religious imagery in the play.
5. What kind of people led the city-states in Italy?
6. Write a one-sentence definition of 'patriarchal'.
7. Why might Capulet be keen for his daughter to marry Paris?
8. Name the two characters who are killed on the streets of Verona.
9. In which setting do Romeo and Juliet declare their love?
10. Who runs away from the tomb at the end of the play?

Power paragraphs

Choose one key setting or contextual idea from the play. Write **two paragraphs** explaining how Shakespeare makes dramatic use of this setting or context in relation to either a) character or b) theme.

My progress   Needs more work ☐   Getting there ☐   Sorted! ☐

...gs about Romeo in Acts I and II

1. ...sensitive and **more serious** than some of his friends.
2. ... **prone to fall in love easily** and **acts with his heart** rather than his head.
3. He keeps his relationship with Juliet **secret** and **places his trust** in the Friar, seeking **his advice**.
4. He is **honourable** in his promises to Juliet.
5. He **marries Juliet in secret** at Friar Lawrence's cell.

What do we learn about Romeo at the beginning of the play?

- Romeo is the only son of the Montague family.
- He is not involved in the initial fight between the feuding families.
- He is infatuated with a girl called Rosaline who, as he tells his friend Benvolio, does not return his love.
- He has a bad feeling about attending the Capulet feast.
- He is brave in pursuing Juliet when he finds out she is a Capulet.

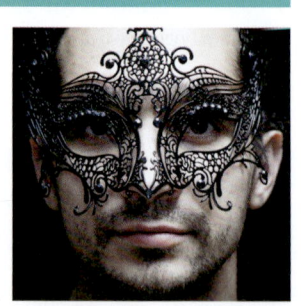

How does Romeo's character develop?

- Romeo's feelings of infatuation for Rosaline at the beginning of the play show his lovesick nature. (Act I)
- He reveals he is intuitive and sensitive and not as light-hearted as some of the other Montague young men. (Act I)
- His feelings for Rosaline fade away quickly when he meets Juliet. (Act I)
- We see hints of his reckless side when he climbs into the Capulet orchard, knowing this is dangerous. (Act II)
- He shows he can be committed to Juliet and serious about marriage and is not just a lovesick and fickle youth. (Act II)

CHARACTERS Romeo in Acts I and II

Five key quotations

1. Romeo, lovesick for Rosaline: **'Love is a smoke made with the fume of sighs'** (I.1.184)
2. Showing his serious and sad side to Mercutio: **'You have dancing shoes/ With nimble soles, I have a soul of lead'** (I.4.14–15)
3. On first sight of Juliet: **'O she doth teach the torches to burn bright!/ It seems she hangs upon the cheek of night/As a rich jewel in an Ethiop's ear'** (I.5.43–5)
4. In the orchard: **'I have night's cloak to hide me from their eyes,/And but thou love me, let them find me here'** (II.2.75–6)
5. Serious side, keeping his promise to Juliet: **'And there she shall at Friar Lawrence's cell/Be shriv'd and married'** (II.4.165–6)

Note it!

Note how when Tybalt is enraged at Romeo's presence at the feast, Capulet comments **'Verona brags of him/To be a virtuous and well-governed youth.'** If the lovers had been honest with their parents, perhaps the tragedy could have been avoided.

Exam focus

How can I write about Romeo as a sensitive character? AO1

You can write about your first impressions of Romeo.

> In the early part of the play, Romeo is presented as sensitive and a character who falls in love easily and desperately. He is captivated when he first sees Juliet, who is so beautiful, she doth teach the torches to burn bright!' in his eyes. This reveals his romantic nature and how he is open to love. He seems very different to some of the young men in the play, who are bawdy and violent.

- Clearly identifies Romeo's key characteristics
- Supported by an example of Romeo's dialogue
- An inference to make a contrasting follow-up point

Now you try!

Finish this paragraph about Romeo. Use one of the quotations from the list above.

However, we see a serious side to Romeo when ....

My progress — Needs more work ☐ Getting there ☐ Sorted! ☐

31

CHARACTERS Romeo in Acts III–V

Five key things about Romeo in Acts III–V

1. **Romeo** tries to **keep the peace** when Tybalt challenges the Montagues.
2. He is **devastated** by **Mercutio's death** and **seeks revenge** from **Tybalt**.
3. **Romeo** feels great anguish when he is **banished from Verona** for **killing Tybalt**.
4. **Romeo** spends **one night with Juliet** before leaving for **Mantua**.
5. He rushes back to **Verona, mistakenly believing Juliet** to be **dead**.

How does Romeo's character develop?

- Romeo's peaceful nature is overridden when he sees Mercutio killed and he is driven to revenge, killing Tybalt. (Act III)
- He is driven to panic and distress when he learns of his banishment. (Act III)
- He is strong and supportive to Juliet when he is forced to leave her after their wedding night. (Act III)
- He shows his desperation by persuading the apothecary to sell him poison before he returns to Verona. (Act V)
- He acts in haste and without full knowledge of the situation when he rushes back to Verona and the Capulet tomb, killing Paris and himself before Juliet wakes. (Act V)

What do we learn about Romeo by the end of the play?

- Romeo's initial instincts are to be a peacemaker, but he is driven to rash behaviour.
- He is loyal and honourable to his friend Mercutio.
- He sees banishment as being worse than death if he cannot be with Juliet.
- He can be both tender and brave when he takes his leave from Juliet.
- Romeo's final acts prove, but with tragic consequences, that his love for Juliet was deep and genuine.

CHARACTERS Romeo in Acts III–V

Five key quotations

1. Romeo trying to keep the peace with Tybalt: 'I do protest I never injured thee,/But love thee better than thou canst devise' (III.1.65–6)
2. After Tybalt's death: 'O, I am fortune's fool' (III.1.132)
3. Comforting Juliet as he leaves: 'all these woes shall serve/For sweet discourses in our times to come' (II.5.52–3)
4. Buying the poison: 'Come, cordial and not poison, go with me/To Juliet's grave, for there must I use thee' (V.1.85–6)
5. Finding Juliet in the tomb: 'O my love, my wife,/Death, that hath suck'd the honey of thy breath,/Hath had no power yet upon thy beauty' (V.3.91–3)

Note it!

Note how Romeo can move swiftly between being sensitive and tender and then acting hastily and without thought. He is quick to panic and acts in haste without the guidance of the Friar to calm him and make him see reason.

Exam focus

How can I write about Romeo as impetuous and hasty? AO1

You can write about Romeo's actions later in the play.

Though Romeo is aiming to keep the peace, **he is driven to act in revenge for Mercutio's death without thinking of the consequences.** Only afterwards does he realise his tragic mistake and he cries, **'O, I am fortune's fool'.** Not only does Romeo seem capable of acting in the same violent way as Mercutio and Tybalt, he is acknowledging how he has been a 'fool' to act so hastily and has allowed himself to be a victim of fate.

- Shows insight into the plot
- Supports with a key quotation
- Makes an inference connecting Romeo to other characters
- Develops the analysis by focusing on key words in the supporting quotation

Now you try!

Finish this paragraph about Romeo, showing his more gentle side at this point in the play. Use one of the quotations from the list above.

Romeo can also be seen to be loving and supportive when he takes his leave of ....

My progress   Needs more work ☐   Getting there ☐   Sorted! ☐

CHARACTERS Juliet in Acts I and II

Five key things about Juliet in Acts I and II

1. **Capulet** and **Paris** discuss **Juliet's future** before we even meet her.
2. She has a **trusting relationship** with her **Nurse** at this point in the play.
3. **Juliet's relationship** with her **mother** seems **more cold and distant**.
4. **Juliet** is **young and innocent** but she is also **strong-willed and independent**.
5. **Juliet** is **instantly attracted** to **Romeo** at the **feast** and is **determined** to **marry** him.

What do we learn about Juliet at the beginning of the play?

- Juliet is the only living child of the Capulet household.
- She is very young and has been brought up by her Nurse.
- She is asked to consider marriage to the wealthy and handsome Paris.
- At the feast she is instantly attracted to Romeo, rather than Paris.
- Juliet, not Romeo, is the first to mention marriage.

How does Juliet's character develop?

- At first Juliet seems willing to respect her parents' wishes for a marriage to Paris. (Act I)
- Her interaction with Romeo at the feast shows she is quick-witted and clever. (Act I)
- She falls in love quickly with Romeo and when he visits the orchard, she seems determined and open in expressing her feelings for him. (Act II)
- Juliet places her trust in the Nurse and sends her to meet Romeo. (Act II)
- Despite being respectful on the surface to her parents, Juliet marries Romeo without their knowledge. (Act II)

CHARACTERS Juliet in Acts I and II

Five key quotations

1. Juliet on meeting Paris at the feast: **'I'll look to like, if looking liking move'** (I.3.98)
2. At the feast with Romeo: **'You kiss by th' book'** (I.5.109)
3. On discovering Romeo is a Montague: **'Tis but thy name that is my enemy;/Thou art thyself, though not a Montague'** (II.2.38–9)
4. Impatient for news of Romeo: **'What says he of our marriage, what of that?'** (II.5.47)
5. Juliet, about to marry Romeo: **'But my true love is grown to such excess/I cannot sum up sum of half my wealth'** (II.6.33–4)

Note it!

Think about why Juliet mentions marriage to Romeo so quickly. Consider whether she is as keen, after the feast, to avoid an arranged marriage to Paris as she is to marry Romeo.

Exam focus

How can I write about Juliet at the start of the play? AO1 AO2

You can write about how Juliet shows different sides to her character.

At the beginning of the play, Juliet seems young and naïve. However, she is also clever and headstrong. — *Point introduces contrasting sides of character*

When she meets Romeo she finds witty ways to justify a future with him, through word play with Romeo's name. She seems to debate the idea, — *Develops into a language point*

considering, 'Tis but thy name that is my enemy;/ Thou art thyself, though not a Montague.' — *Strong supporting quotation*

Shakespeare shows how she dismisses the danger of family feud lightly and considers how she might still be able to love him. — *Makes an inference about Juliet's actions*

Now you try!

Finish this paragraph discussing Juliet's impatience to marry Romeo. Use one of the quotations from the list above.

Shakespeare shows us how Juliet can behave in a way that is ....

My progress Needs more work ☐ Getting there ☐ Sorted! ☐

CHARACTERS Juliet in Acts III–V

Five key things about Juliet in Acts III–V

1. **Juliet** shows the **depth of her love** for **Romeo** during her soliloquy in Act III.
2. Despite the news of **Tybalt's death**, **Juliet** is determined to **remain faithful** to **Romeo**.
3. **Juliet** is, however, **capable of deceiving** those closest to her – **her parents** and the Nurse.
4. She is **courageous** in going ahead with the plan to **fake her death**.
5. She is **let down by Friar Lawrence** who runs away, leaving **Juliet** with Romeo's body to **take her own life**.

How does Juliet's character develop?

- Juliet shows conflicting feelings when she learns of Tybalt's death but maintains her loyalty to Romeo. (Act III)
- She experiences anxiety when she learns of Romeo's banishment and is ready to take her own life. (Act IV)
- She is a good actress and convinces her parents and the Nurse she is ready and willing to marry Paris. (Act IV)
- By taking the potion and, later, by taking her own life, she shows her desperation to be with Romeo and her deep love for him. (Acts IV and V)

What do we learn about Juliet by the end of the play?

- Despite her attempt at independence, Juliet's future is still governed by her father.
- She is headstrong and passionate.
- She is placed in a morally impossible situation in having to marry Paris, when she is already married.
- She is willing to place herself in danger and take a risk to be reunited with Romeo.
- She makes a mistake in trusting both the Nurse and the Friar.

CHARACTERS Juliet in Acts III–V

Five key quotations

1. Juliet waiting for Romeo: **'Romeo/Leap to these arms, untalk'd of and unseen'** (III.2.6–7)
2. On learning that Romeo has killed Tybalt: **'Beautiful tyrant, fiend angelical!'** (III.2.75)
3. Defying her parents over the arranged marriage: **'He shall not make me there a joyful bride'** (III.5.117)
4. Deceiving her parents and the Nurse: **'I have learnt me to repent the sin/Of disobedient opposition/To you and your behests'** (IV.2.17–19)
5. On discovering Romeo's body in the tomb: **'I will kiss thy lips,/Haply some poison yet doth hang on them,/To make me die with a restorative'** (V.3.164–7)

Note it!

Note how Juliet's loyalties lie with Romeo once she marries him. Though she is upset about Tybalt, her distress for Romeo's banishment is more overwhelming. She also disregards the Nurse's advice to go through with the second marriage to Paris.

Exam focus

How can I write about Juliet's deception? AO1

You can write about how Juliet is forced to deceive her loved ones.

> Juliet is forced to deceive both the Nurse and her parents once she realises the marriage to Paris has been arranged without her consent. She states she has, 'learnt me to repent the sin/Of disobedient opposition' whilst all the time the audience are aware she has plotted a means of escape with the Friar, not gone to him to pray for forgiveness.

- Clear statement focusing on Juliet's deception
- Embeds a relevant quotation
- Considers the impact on the audience

Now you try!

Finish this paragraph exploring Juliet's loyalty to her husband. Use one of the quotations from the list above.

Shakespeare presents Juliet as capable of feeling ....

My progress — Needs more work ☐ Getting there ☐ Sorted! ☐

CHARACTERS Mercutio and Tybalt

Three key things about Mercutio

1. **Mercutio** is **kinsman** to the **Prince**, a **Montague** and **Romeo's friend**.
2. He is very **lively, quick-witted and changeable**.
3. He can be **hot headed** and is **easily provoked** when the Capulets start fighting on the streets.

What is his function in the play?

- Mercutio acts as a light-hearted contrast to Romeo's seriousness, especially on the topic of love and dreams, which he shows through the playful and riddling style of his 'Queen Mab' speech.
- His rage and hot temper prompt the duel with Tybalt in place of Romeo and then his death.
- Mercutio's death is the catalyst for Romeo to seek revenge and leads to him killing Tybalt.

Three key things about Tybalt

1. **Tybalt** is **Juliet's fiery cousin**.
2. He is the character who **instigates the fighting** in the **opening scene**.
3. He often uses **language** filled with **hatred** and is **easily insulted, angered** and **provoked**.

What is his function in the play?

- Tybalt represents the violent and vengeful nature of society in Verona and shows how feuding and rivalry can both divide and be dangerous.
- He is a contrast to Benvolio and Romeo who both try to keep the peace.
- His death in Act III creates the consequence that causes Romeo's banishment and brings forward Juliet's marriage to Paris.

CHARACTERS Mercutio and Tybalt

Five key quotations

1. Mercutio, on his imaginings: 'I talk of dreams,/Which are the children of an idle brain' (I.4.96–7)
2. Mercutio, taking up Romeo's challenge: 'O calm, dishonourable, vile submission! ... Tybalt, you rat-catcher, will you walk?' (III.1.70–2)
3. As he lies dying, Mercutio's words to Romeo: 'A plague a'both your houses! ... Why the dev'l came you between us! I was hurt under your arm' (III.1.95–9)
4. Tybalt to Benvolio as he tries to keep the peace: 'What, drawn and talk of peace? I hate the word,/As I hate hell, all Montagues, and thee' (I.1.64–5)
5. Tybalt at Capulet's feast: 'This, by his voice, should be a Montague./Fetch me my rapier, boy' (I.5.53–4)

Note it!

Note how both Mercutio and Tybalt are easily angered and quick to respond with violence. They show how family honour was defended in Veronese society and how life could be dangerous, brutal and end prematurely.

Exam focus

How can I write about Mercutio's character? AO1 AO2

You can comment on how Shakespeare uses Mercutio for swift changes in the pace of the action.

> Mercutio is often seen as a lively and humorous character in the play. However he has a changeable nature and is swift to respond when the Montagues are challenged by Tybalt. He sees Romeo's reluctance as a 'calm, dishonourable vile submission!' and in acting hastily does not stop to consider whether Romeo had good reason for keeping the peace.

- Shows knowledge of character and plot
- Selective use of quotation
- Makes a thoughtful comment

Now you try!

Finish this paragraph by making a comparison with Tybalt. Use one of the quotations from the list above.

In this way, Mercutio could be seen as having some similarities with Tybalt ....

My progress   Needs more work ☐   Getting there ☐   Sorted! ☐

CHARACTERS Lord and Lady Capulet

Three key things about Lord Capulet

1. **Lord Capulet** is **Juliet's father**. At first he **seems caring and concerned** that she does not marry too young.
2. He is the **head of a wealthy Veronese household** and all of the decision-making rests on him – including who his daughter will marry.
3. Though he **seems jovial and sociable**, he can also be **domineering, easily angered and cruel**.

What is his function in the play?

- Capulet represents a patriarchal society and his behaviour reveals how at this time a woman's future was governed by her father and husband.
- His change of heart when he agrees to Juliet's marriage with Paris quickens the pace of the action in the play.
- His angry response to Juliet's refusal leads to her taking desperate measures to avoid the second wedding.

Three key things about Lady Capulet

1. **Lady Capulet** is **married to Lord Capulet** and is **Juliet's mother**. She is probably much younger than her husband.
2. Lady Capulet seems **happier** than her husband for Juliet to marry young, realising perhaps that this is the only way to a **secure future** for her daughter.
3. She appears **rather cold** and **emotionless** throughout the play and she ultimately **supports her husband** rather than Juliet.

What is her function in the play?

- Lady Capulet represents the life of a wealthy upper-class woman who has not spent much time with her child.
- She contrasts with the Nurse who seems to have a closer and warmer relationship with Juliet.
- Shakespeare uses her to show how marriage was more a practical business transaction than a love match in the way she presents Paris's offer to Juliet.

CHARACTERS Lord and Lady Capulet

Five key quotations

1. Capulet advising Paris: **'But woo her, gentle Paris, get her heart,/My will to her consent is but a part'** (I.2.16–17)
2. Capulet changing his mind about the marriage to Paris: **'Go you to Juliet ere you go to bed,/Prepare her, wife, against this wedding day'** (III.4.31–2)
3. Capulet enraged by Juliet's refusal: **'fettle your fine joints 'gainst Thursday next,/To go with Paris to Saint Peter's Church,/Or I will drag thee'** (III.5.153–5)
4. Lady Capulet discussing marriage with Juliet: **'Well, think of marriage now; younger than you,/Here in Verona, ladies of esteem,/Are made already mothers'** (I.3.70–2)
5. Lady Capulet dismissing Juliet's pleas: **'Talk not to me, for I'll not speak a word./Do as thou wilt, for I have done with thee'** (III.5.202–3)

Note it!

Think about the way Capulet treats both his wife and daughter. Lady Capulet seems almost afraid to cross him and he gives Juliet no chance to explain. She realises that if he goes back on his word to Paris, he will be dishonoured.

Exam focus

How can I write about Capulet's character? AO1 AO2

You can comment on the way Shakespeare presents Capulet as a figure of authority.

> After Tybalt's death, Capulet mistakenly believes a wedding would help Juliet to overcome her grief. ==He shows his authority in the household by deciding for her and issuing orders using imperatives to his wife== to 'Prepare her, wife, against this wedding day.' This hasty decision helps us understand how little Capulet really knows his daughter and how lacking in sensitivity he is.

- Clear point about the character's actions
- Quotation supports the point
- Thoughtful comment and inference about character

Now you try!

Finish this paragraph about Lady Capulet. Use one of the quotations from the list above.

In Act III, Lady Capulet speaks to Juliet in a way that is ....

My progress   Needs more work ☐   Getting there ☐   Sorted! ☐

CHARACTERS The Nurse and Friar Lawrence

Three key things about the Nurse

1. The **Nurse** has **brought up Juliet** and is the person **closest to her** in the Capulet household.
2. She **loves talking** and has a **bawdy sense of humour**.
3. She is **keen to see Juliet married** and happy, but her advice can be **changeable and unreliable**.

What is her function in the play?

- The Nurse is presented as a contrast to Juliet's mother; whereas her mother is distant and cold, the Nurse is affectionate towards Juliet.
- She is the intermediary between Juliet and Romeo, carrying messages and making arrangements for the lovers to meet and marry.
- She eventually betrays Juliet's trust and confidence by suggesting she marry Paris after Romeo's banishment, leaving Juliet isolated and willing to take drastic risks on her own.

Three key things about Friar Lawrence

1. **Friar Lawrence** has taken holy orders and is therefore able to **marry the two lovers**.
2. He is Romeo's **trusted friend** and **adviser**.
3. A **skilled herbalist**, he makes medicines and potions from the plants and herbs he collects.

What is his function in the play?

- The Friar performs the marriage service for Romeo and Juliet believing it will help to heal the Capulet–Montague feud.
- He advises and calms Romeo after he has been banished and has a plan to help the couple reunite in the future.
- He prepares the drug which will allow Juliet to fake her death.
- He is responsible for sending a message to Romeo. His panic at the end of the play means he fails to communicate his plan for Juliet to Romeo in time.

CHARACTERS The Nurse and Friar Lawrence

Five key quotations

1. The Nurse as Juliet prepares for the feast: **'Go, girl, seek happy nights to happy days'** (I.3.106)
2. The Nurse advising Juliet about the arranged marriage to Paris: **'Then since the case so stands as now it doth,/I think it best you married with the County'** (III.5.216–17)
3. The Friar learning of Romeo's love for Juliet: **'In one respect I'll thy assistant be:/For this alliance may so happy prove/To turn your households' rancour to pure love.'** (II.3.90–2)
4. The Friar revealing his plan to Juliet: **'I do spy a kind of hope,/Which craves as desperate an execution/As that is desperate which we would prevent'** (IV.1.68–70)
5. The Friar's final cowardice in leaving Juliet: **'I dare no longer stay'** (V.3.159)

Note it!

Note how the Nurse advises Juliet to marry Paris – though this would be a sin as she is already married to Romeo. The Friar, when Juliet wakes in the tomb, offers to take her to a convent. It is possible they are both trying to protect themselves after their earlier ill-judged actions.

Exam focus

How can I write about the Nurse's character? AO1

You can write about how the Nurse is used as a contrast.

> One of the functions of the Nurse is to contrast with Lady Capulet in the way she cares for Juliet. At the prospect of meeting Paris the Nurse advises her to 'Go, girl, seek happy nights to happy days.' The Nurse, having cared for Juliet since she was a baby, focuses on Juliet's future happiness. This is very different from the way Lady Capulet views the match.

- Quotation embedded well in key point
- Detailed knowledge of the character
- Inference showing knowledge about another character

Now you try!

Finish this paragraph about the Friar. Use one of the quotations from the list above.

Similarly, one of the Friar's functions in the play is to advise ....

My progress   Needs more work ☐   Getting there ☐   Sorted! ☐

CHARACTERS Benvolio and Paris

Three key things about Benvolio

1. **Benvolio** is a member of the **Montague** family.
2. His name means **'I wish (or mean) well'**.
3. In the play he is often seen **keeping the peace** or being kind to Romeo.

What is his function in the play?

- Benvolio is presented as a mature, sensible character and advises the other young Montague men against violence.
- He is seen as a loyal friend to Romeo and listens sensitively to his problems.
- He represents a contrast to both Tybalt and Mercutio who are more hot-headed and fiery.

Three key things about Paris

1. **Paris** is a young, **wealthy Count** from a noble family.
2. He **wishes to marry Juliet** and asks her father for her hand.
3. He **visits Juliet's tomb** to bring flowers and is **killed by Romeo**.

What is his function in the play?

- Paris shows how, at the time the play was written, marriages were arranged between the suitor and the bride's father.
- He represents wealth and security to Lady Capulet and a way for Juliet to elevate her status.
- He also represents **courtly love** traditions in that he seeks Juliet's love when she is not interested in him.
- Paris contributes to **dramatic irony**: he is killed never knowing about Romeo's marriage to Juliet and of his real purpose in coming to the Capulet tomb.

CHARACTERS Benvolio and Paris

Five key quotations

1. Benvolio preventing a fight between the Montagues and Capulets: **'Put up your swords, you know not what you do'** (I.1.58–9)
2. Benvolio trying to prevent further fighting: **'I pray thee, good Mercutio, let's retire;/The day is hot, the Capels are abroad'** (III.1.1–2)
3. Paris visiting the Capulets after Tybalt's death: **'These times of woe afford no times to woo,/Madam, good night, commend me to your daughter'** (III.4.8–9)
4. Paris finding Juliet at the Friar's cell: **'Happily met, my lady and my wife!'** (IV.1.18)
5. Paris visiting Juliet's body in the Capulet tomb: **'Sweet flower, with flowers thy bridal bed I strew—'** (V.3.12)

Note it!
Note how Shakespeare uses both Benvolio and Paris to contrast with more quick-tempered characters. Their measured behaviour also contrasts with Romeo's hasty actions and the spontaneous way he falls in love.

Exam focus

How can I write about Benvolio's character? AO1 AO2

You can comment on how Benvolio is used to communicate a message about peace instead of violence.

In the play we see violence and hear of 'brawls' in the streets of Verona. **Benvolio always appears to use mature language and be ready to speak sense and reason,** 'I pray thee, good Mercutio, let's retire;/The day is hot, the Capels are abroad'. He shows the better judgement of the Montagues and **perhaps is used to hint how the feud could have easily been resolved with good sense rather than causing the tragedy we witness.**	Clear statement about character Supports with an apt quotation Thoughtful inference about function of the character

Now you try!

Finish this paragraph about Paris. Use one of the quotations from the list above.

Similarly, Paris is presented as a sensitive ....

My progress Needs more work ☐ Getting there ☐ Sorted! ☐

CHARACTERS Quick revision

1. Look at this timeline representing Romeo's character development throughout the play. Can you decide which quotation (A–E) matches each point in his development?

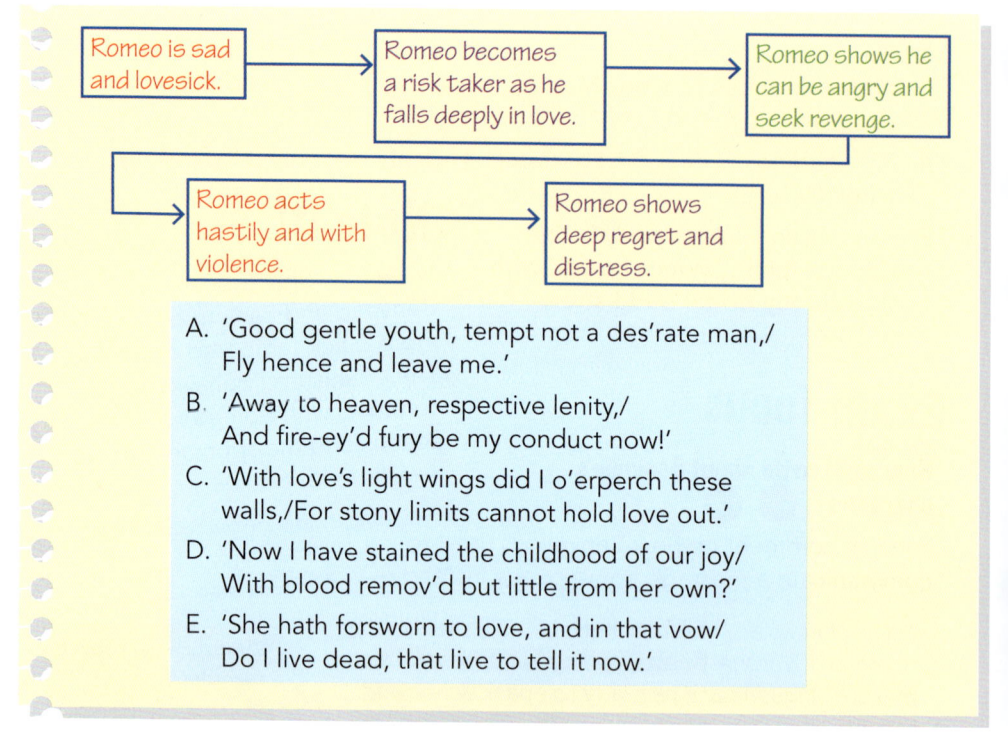

> Romeo is sad and lovesick. → Romeo becomes a risk taker as he falls deeply in love. → Romeo shows he can be angry and seek revenge.
>
> → Romeo acts hastily and with violence. → Romeo shows deep regret and distress.
>
> A. 'Good gentle youth, tempt not a des'rate man,/ Fly hence and leave me.'
> B. 'Away to heaven, respective lenity,/ And fire-ey'd fury be my conduct now!'
> C. 'With love's light wings did I o'erperch these walls,/For stony limits cannot hold love out.'
> D. 'Now I have stained the childhood of our joy/ With blood remov'd but little from her own?'
> E. 'She hath forsworn to love, and in that vow/ Do I live dead, that live to tell it now.'

2. Create your own timeline for the development of the character of Juliet and select five appropriate quotations to match each point.

Quick quiz

Answer these quick questions about the play's characters.

1. Who is Rosaline?
2. Who holds a feast and why?
3. Which character seeks the hand of Juliet?
4. Who describes Paris as 'a man of wax'?
5. Who is angry that Romeo has come to the Capulet feast?

CHARACTERS Quick revision

6. Which character describes Queen Mab?
7. Who lets Juliet know that Romeo is a Montague?
8. Which character is awake at dawn picking herbs?
9. Who accompanies the Nurse to find Romeo?
10. Who has sent a challenge to the Montagues' house?
11. Who has been waiting for the Nurse since nine in the morning?
12. Who calls Tybalt 'Good King of Cats'?
13. Who calls for Romeo to be put to death after Tybalt is killed?
14. Which character tells Juliet the news of Romeo's banishment?
15. Which character tells Romeo the news that he is banished?
16. Who sends a ring to Romeo?
17. Which character meets Juliet at Friar Lawrence's cell on Tuesday morning?
18. Who stays up all night to prepare for a wedding?
19. Which character discovers Juliet's 'body' on the morning of her wedding?
20. Who does Romeo visit to buy the poison?

Power paragraphs

Write a paragraph in response to each of these questions. For each, use one quotation you have learned from this section.

1. In what ways does Shakespeare contrast Benvolio and Mercutio?
2. Why does Shakespeare choose to include the scene showing Paris visiting the Capulets following Tybalt's death?

Exam practice

Re-read the extract showing Capulet's anger when he learns Juliet does not want to marry Paris (III.5.140–200).

What is revealed here of Capulet's character and his attitude towards his daughter? Write **two paragraphs** explaining your ideas. You could comment on:

- the contrast between his caring behaviour at the beginning of the play and his role as father in a patriarchal society
- his worry that he will not secure the match and family connection with wealthy Paris.

My progress   Needs more work ☐   Getting there ☐   Sorted! ☐

THEMES Love

Five key things about the theme of love

1. **Love** is treated and spoken of in **many different ways** in the play.
2. The play represents **courtly love** traditions through the **lovesick actions** of **Romeo**.
3. Love is also presented as a **distant emotion** through **Paris's proposal to Juliet** which seems to be an **arrangement for status** and increased **power**.
4. This **distance** can also be seen through the **parental love** of the **Capulets** for **Juliet**.
5. **Romantic love** can be seen as **spontaneous** and **dangerous** through the **immediate attraction** of **Romeo** and **Juliet**.

What does love mean to Romeo and Juliet?

- Romeo sees love as something all-consuming and he speaks of both Rosaline and then Juliet in ways that make them seem heavenly or like goddesses.
- Both Romeo and Juliet experience love as a strong emotional and physical attraction to each other.
- Both characters see love as being linked to marriage which they view as the way to make a true vow of love to one another.
- Both characters recognise that their love is dangerous against the backdrop of the family feud.
- Both Romeo and Juliet are prepared to die to protect their love for each other.

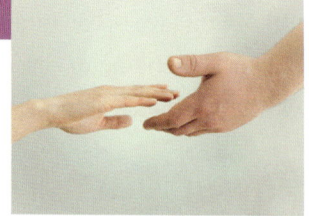

What does love mean to other characters in the play?

- Benvolio sees Romeo's infatuation with Rosaline as too serious and foolish and encourages him to meet other young girls.
- The Nurse views love as being linked with marriage and sexual pleasure.
- Mercutio and the young men of the Capulet household seem to view love only in sexual terms as revealed by the many jokes they make and their use of rough humour.
- Friar Lawrence sees love as being the possible source of reconciliation between the families but warns against the speed and which young people can fall in love.

THEMES Love

Five key quotations

1. Romeo to Mercutio: **'Under love's heavy burden do I sink'** (I.4.22)
2. Juliet on finding out Romeo's identity: **'My only love sprung from my only hate!/Prodigious birth of love it is to me,/That I must love a loathed enemy'** (I.5.137–40)
3. Juliet to Romeo in the orchard: **'O swear not by the moon, th' inconstant moon,/That monthly changes in her circl'd orb,/Lest that thy love prove likewise variable'** (II.2.109–11)
4. Juliet makes her vow to Romeo: **'And yet I wish but for the thing I have:/My bounty is as boundless as the sea'** (II.2.132–3)
5. Friar Lawrence to Romeo: **'These violent delights have violent ends, … Therefore love moderately, long love doth so'** (II.6.9–14)

Note it!

Note how Friar Lawrence warns the young couple about acting in haste once they have fallen in love at first sight. However, he goes on to marry them that same afternoon, in the belief that the marriage may reconcile the feud between the families.

Exam focus

How does Shakespeare present ideas about love? AO1

You can comment on the different ways love is presented depending on a character's situation.

> Shakespeare presents love in different ways. When Romeo is suffering as a result of unrequited love for Rosaline he tells his friends that, 'under love's heavy burden do I sink'. Here love is seen in a negative light as an emotion that is draining and has the potential to cause misery.

- Comments on the writer's use of the theme
- An apt quotation well embedded
- An evaluative comment on the effect of the theme

Now you try!

Finish this paragraph showing a different side to love. Use one of the quotations from the list above.

Shakespeare also shows us that love can be dangerous ....

My progress   Needs more work ☐   Getting there ☐   Sorted! ☐

THEMES Fate and free will

Five key things about the theme of fate and free will

1. The **Prologue** sets up the idea that **fate is to blame** for the tragedy.
2. Both **Romeo** and **Juliet** feel that **fate is working against their relationship** throughout the play.
3. Much of the **language** that Romeo and Juliet use to describe their love is connected to the workings of the **stars and the heavens**.
4. By **acting out of free will**, Romeo and Juliet **challenge the conventions** of their society at the time.
5. Though the plot seems to involve cruel **twists of fate**, many events could have been **prevented** with **less haste and more honesty** from the lovers.

What does fate and free will mean to Romeo and Juliet?

- Romeo senses that attending the Capulet feast will not be a good idea.
- Juliet's strong sense of free will leads her to arrange her own marriage and defy her father's authority.
- Romeo feels he has been tricked by fate when he kills Tybalt in revenge.
- Juliet has a chilling premonition of Romeo's death when he leaves after their wedding night.
- Romeo openly challenges the fates when he hears of Juliet's death, calling out bitterly to the stars and the heavens.

How is fate and free will connected to other characters in the play?

- Benvolio suggests that attending the feast will help Romeo forget Rosaline. His words become a prediction in that Romeo sees Juliet for the first time and his feelings for Rosaline disappear.
- Tybalt tempts fate when he suggests that Romeo will eventually be made to pay for his intrusion at the Capulet feast.
- Many of Friar Lawrence's words have a chilling sense of future events within them, e.g. **'These violent delights have violent ends'**.
- It may seem that fate intervenes to prevent Juliet from marrying Paris.

THEMES Fate and free will

Five key quotations

1. Initial message about fate: **'From forth the fatal loins of these two foes/A pair of star-cross'd lovers take their life'** (Prologue.5–6)
2. Romeo before the Capulet feast: **'Some consequence yet hanging in the stars/Shall bitterly begin his fearful date/With this night's revels'** (I.4.107–9)
3. Romeo, following Mercutio's death: **'This day's black fate on moe days doth depend,/This but begins the woe others must end'** (III.1.115–16)
4. Juliet, as Romeo leaves her at daybreak: **'Methinks I see thee now, thou art low,/As one dead in the bottom of a tomb'** (III.5.55–6)
5. Romeo, learning of Juliet's death: **'I defy you, stars!'** (V.1.24)

Note it!

Note how we are introduced to the lovers, right from the start of the play, as **'star-cross'd'**, as if the heavens have literally preordained their destiny. Consider which of the play's events that appear to be cruel twists of fate could have been prevented.

Exam focus

How does Shakespeare present ideas about fate and free will? AO1

You can comment on the different moments in the play when fate is presented.

Juliet's words when she watches Romeo depart after their wedding night take on a chilling significance as she observes, 'Methinks I see thee now, thou art so low/As one dead in the bottom of a tomb.' However, it is Romeo who finds Juliet 'as one dead' in the Capulet vault and, believing her to be so, kills himself before she revives. This appears in the play as a final dark twist of fate and make Juliet's words here a grim prophecy.

- Locates and comments on a key 'fateful' moment
- Exemplifies with a quotation
- Shows a wider knowledge of the play
- Comments thoughtfully on the theme

Now you try!

Finish this paragraph showing how early in the play Romeo seems to sense fate. Use one of the quotations from the list above.

Shakespeare shows Romeo to believe that fate is shaping his future ....

My progress   Needs more work ☐   Getting there ☐   Sorted! ☐

THEMES Family and marriage

Five key things about the theme of family and marriage

1. Much of the play's **violence** is caused by the idea of **family honour**.
2. The **feud** between the two families is the **obstacle** to Romeo and Juliet's **marriage**.
3. **Marriage** is seen as a way of **maintaining honour** and **increasing status** among the wealthy Veronese families.
4. The **arranged marriage** between Juliet and Paris is **not based on love**; the marriage between **Romeo and Juliet** is **solely based on love**.
5. **Juliet's family** is **ruled by Capulet** who makes all the decisions and **heads the household**.

What does family and marriage mean to Romeo and Juliet?

- The conflict between the couple's families is at the back of their minds from the moment they learn each other's names.
- Marriage in front of God is important to the two of them and they make formal vows so their families cannot separate them.
- Juliet marries Romeo knowing her father is in the process of arranging a marriage to Paris, suggesting she does this to avoid the match.
- Romeo quickly makes a firm commitment of marriage to Juliet to prove he is honourable towards her.
- Their marriage is short-lived but filled with love and passion.

What does family and marriage mean to other characters in the play?

- Paris seeks Juliet's hand in a formal way, matching the social conventions of the time.
- Capulet sees it as a father's duty to find the right husband for his daughter.
- Lady Capulet sees marriage as a way for her daughter to gain wealth, security and status. She does not consider the importance of love.
- Tybalt is fiercely proud of his family's honour and provokes much of the play's violence to defend it.
- The Montagues and Capulets reconcile their differences only when they realise Romeo and Juliet had married.

THEMES Family and marriage

Five key quotations

1. Depth of family feud: **'Two households, both alike in dignity ... From ancient grudge break to new mutiny'** (Prologue.1–4)
2. Juliet, on learning Romeo is a Montague: **'O Romeo, Romeo, wherefore art thou Romeo?/Deny thy father and refuse thy name'** (II.2.33–4)
3. Juliet, learning of Tybalt's death: **'Shall I speak ill of him that is my husband? Ah, poor my lord, what tongue shall smooth thy name'** (III.2.97–8)
4. Capulet, hearing of Juliet's refusal of Paris: **'it makes me mad!/Day, night, work, play,/Alone, in company, still my care hath been/To have her match'd'** (III.5.176–8)
5. The Friar on the discovery of Juliet's 'dead' body: **'She's not well married that lives married long/ But she's best married that dies married young.'** (IV.5.77–8)

Note it!

Lady Capulet is business-like when encouraging Juliet to marry: **'I was your mother much upon these years'**. Later, she shows no pity towards her daughter when she is distressed about marrying Paris.

Exam focus

How can I write about family and marriage? (AO1)

You can comment on the ways marriage is presented by considering how different characters respond to it.

Juliet is fiercely determined to defend Romeo when she learns he has killed Tybalt. She exclaims to her Nurse, 'Shall I speak ill of him that is my husband? Ah, poor my lord, what tongue shall smooth thy name'. This suggests that now married, she places her husband before her family. At this point the audience may be convinced of how genuine and deep her love for Romeo is as she pledges her loyalty to him here.

- Introduces theme of marriage and what it means
- Carefully selected quotation
- Links inference to a key point about theme
- A further thoughtful inference

Now you try!

Finish this paragraph showing how a different character responds to marriage. Use one of the quotations from the list above.

Shakespeare shows us a different attitude towards marriage when Capulet ....

My progress   Needs more work ☐   Getting there ☐   Sorted! ☐

THEMES Conflict and honour

Five key things about the themes of conflict and honour

1. The entire play is set against the **backdrop of the conflict** between the **Capulet and Montague families**.
2. **Family honour** is seen to be important to both **wealthy families** and at times is placed above a regard for life.
3. The Prince warns from the outset that **further conflict** between the families will lead to **serious consequences**.
4. Both **Romeo and Juliet** experience **internal conflict** when they decide to **marry** without their families' knowledge.
5. The conflict **Tybalt** provokes is the *climax* in the *tragedy*.

What do conflict and honour mean to Romeo and Juliet?

- Both Romeo and Juliet are conscious that conflict could occur if they are found together, for example when Romeo is in the Capulet orchard.
- Romeo honours his promise to Juliet to marry her.
- Romeo becomes drawn into the conflict with Tybalt when Mercutio dies.
- Juliet feels conflicted when she learns of Tybalt's death.
- Juliet faces an internal conflict when she is asked to marry Paris for she is already married to Romeo.

What do conflict and honour mean to other characters in the play?

- Paris appears to be honourable in his intentions towards Juliet.
- Capulet is enraged that his family honour will be tarnished by the street fighting and Juliet's refusal of Paris. Honour comes at the expense of his child's happiness and eventually her life.
- Mercutio finds it intolerable that Romeo will not defend family honour against Tybalt. However, as a consequence of this he loses his life.
- Benvolio appears to behave honourably throughout.
- The Nurse and Friar Lawrence give conflicting advice to the young couple and behave less than honourably by leaving them isolated.

THEMES Conflict and honour

Five key quotations

1. Tybalt, in the initial brawl: **'What, drawn and talk of peace? I hate the word,/As I hate hell, all Montagues, and thee'** (I.1.64–5)
2. The Nurse, to Juliet at the feast: **'His name is Romeo, and a Montague/The only son of your great enemy.'** (I.5.135–6)
3. The Friar: **'These violent delights have violent ends'** (II.6.9)
4. Romeo, following Mercutio's death: **'My very friend, hath got his mortal hurt/In my behalf; my reputation stain'd/With Tybalt's slander'** (III.1.106–8)
5. Capulet enraged by Juliet: **'Unworthy as she is, that we have wrought/So worthy a gentleman to be her bride?'** (III.5.144–5)

Note it!

Note how each family is compelled to use violence to defend its honour. Despite being warned of the consequences by the Prince, their behaviour could be seen as less than honourable.

Exam focus

How does Shakespeare present ideas about conflict and honour? AO1 AO3

You can comment on the way a particular character views honour.

> Romeo, who has been seen trying to keep the peace, is drawn into the conflict when he sees his friend murdered in his place: 'My very friend, hath got his mortal hurt/In my behalf; my reputation stain'd/With Tybalt's slander'. It seems as though Romeo's only course of action is to seek revenge, despite the Prince's earlier decree. Family honour seems to be more important than the law in Veronese society.

- Uses a key quotation
- Makes a clear inference showing a knowledge of the plot
- Makes a link to the possible social context

Now you try!

Finish this paragraph showing how a different character views honour. Use one of the quotations from the list above.

Another character for whom honour is important is Tybalt. However, ...

My progress   Needs more work ☐   Getting there ☐   Sorted! ☐

55

THEMES Quick revision

1. Look at this ideas map showing where in the play we see evidence of the **theme** of love. Can you add anything to the blank spaces?

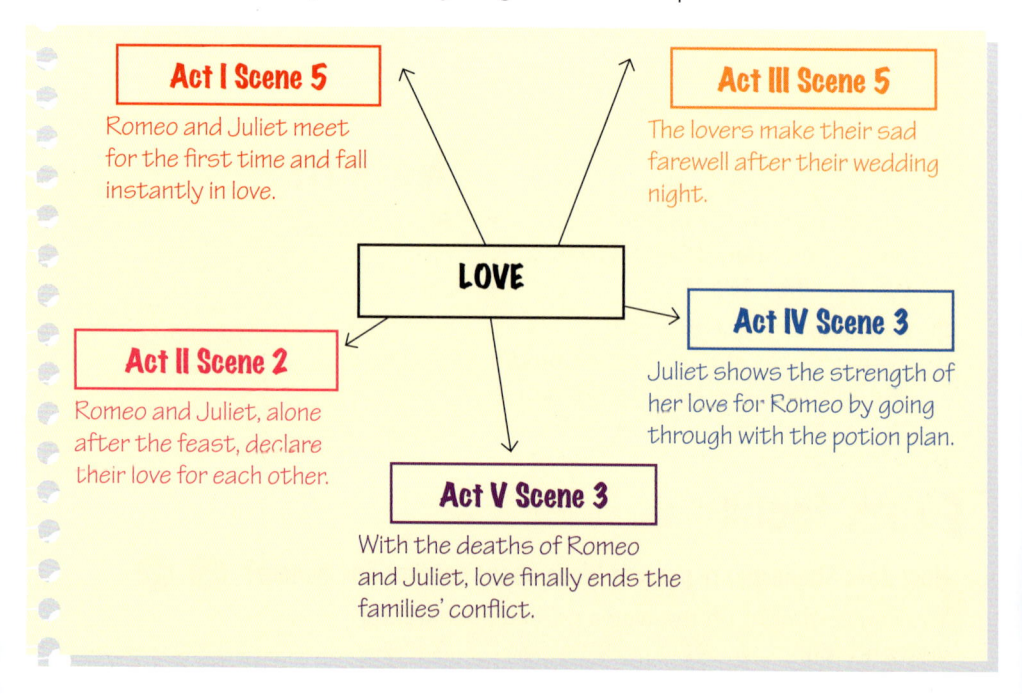

Act I Scene 5
Romeo and Juliet meet for the first time and fall instantly in love.

Act III Scene 5
The lovers make their sad farewell after their wedding night.

LOVE

Act II Scene 2
Romeo and Juliet, alone after the feast, declare their love for each other.

Act IV Scene 3
Juliet shows the strength of her love for Romeo by going through with the potion plan.

Act V Scene 3
With the deaths of Romeo and Juliet, love finally ends the families' conflict.

2. Compile an ideas map for another key theme.

Quick quiz

Answer these quick questions about the themes in the play.

1. Whose fates are seemingly written in the stars at the beginning of the play?
2. Who shows free will in choosing her husband?
3. Which character feels uneasy about going to the feast?
4. Who feels that Juliet is too young for marriage?
5. Who is Romeo's mother?
6. To which family does Mercutio belong?
7. Who provokes the first conflict in the street?

THEMES Quick revision

8. Who encourages Juliet to marry again even though she is married to Romeo?
9. Who fights for the Montague family honour in place of Romeo?
10. Which character tries to avoid conflict at the beginning of Act III?
11. Which character has worked for the Capulet family since Juliet was a baby?
12. Who was married at a similar age to Juliet?
13. Which character describes himself as 'fortune's fool'?
14. Which character says, 'My only love sprung from my only hate'?
15. What punishment does the Prince threaten if more conflict happens in the streets of Verona?
16. Who asks Juliet if she could love Paris before she has even met him?
17. Who feels that marriage could help to solve the family feud?
18. Where do Romeo and Juliet get married?
19. Who else dies of grief because of Romeo's banishment?
20. How many brawls in total have disturbed the peace in Verona?

Power paragraphs

Write a paragraph in response to **each of these questions**. For each, try to **use one quotation** you have learned from this section.
1. How does Shakespeare present Lord and Lady Capulet as parents?
2. By acting out of free will, how do Romeo and Juliet put themselves in great danger?

Exam practice

Re-read the section in Act III when Mercutio answers Tybalt's challenge (III.1.70–130).

Why is this moment significant in the text as a whole? Write **two paragraphs** explaining your ideas. You could comment on:
- the way the two men view family honour
- the consequences of their actions for Romeo and Juliet.

My progress   Needs more work ☐   Getting there ☐   Sorted! ☐

LANGUAGE Imagery and symbolism

Five key things about Shakespeare's use of imagery and symbolism

1. **Shakespeare** uses many **images** that **oppose** or **contrast** with each other.
2. **Similes** and **metaphors** of **light and dark** occur frequently.
3. References to **poison and disease** are often introduced.
4. Shakespeare uses **images of death** to create tension as the play progresses.
5. **Religious images** and **symbols** occur often in the play.

How does Shakespeare use oxymoron, opposites and contrast?

- Shakespeare uses opposites to show the consequences of the feud between the two families, **'O brawling love, O loving hate'**.
- Juliet uses opposites when she hears how her gentle lover has murdered her cousin in revenge, **'Beautiful tyrant, fiend angelical!'**

How does Shakespeare use simile and metaphor in the play?

- Shakespeare creates many images of light to represent the lovers and their feelings for one another, e.g. when Romeo feels that Juliet **'doth teach the torches to burn bright!'**
- Juliet makes comparisons with the heavens, e.g. when she asks the night to **'cut him out in little stars,/And he will make the face of heaven so fine'**.
- Darkness often represents the danger the lovers are in, e.g. when Romeo needs **'night's cloak to hide me from their eyes'**.

How does Shakespeare use imagery and symbolism to build tension?

- Potions and poison become symbolic as the means by which the two lovers can be reunited, e.g. Friar Lawrence speaks of the power of the **'weak flower'**.
- From the start of the play, images of death are presented as a tragic consequence, e.g. when the Prince warns, **'Your lives shall pay the forfeit of the peace.'**
- Shakespeare uses Friar Lawrence's cell as a symbol of safety for Romeo and Juliet, whereas the Capulet tomb comes to symbolise their tragic deaths.

LANGUAGE Imagery and symbolism

Five key quotations

1. Metaphor, describing Juliet's eyes: **'Two of the fairest stars in all the heaven'** (II.2.15)
2. Metaphor, describing Juliet: **'O speak again, bright angel'** (II.2.26)
3. Metaphor, describing Romeo: **'O serpent heart, hid with a flow'ring face!'** (III.2.73)
4. Images of potions from Friar Lawrence: **'I must upfill this osier cage of ours/With baleful weeds and precious-juiced flowers'** (II.3.7–8)
5. Symbolism of the tomb from Juliet: **'Where for this many hundred years the bones/Of all my buried ancestors are pack'd'** (IV.3.40–1)

Note it!
The use of opposing images reminds us of the pull in the play between right and wrong, love and hate, youth and age and the two families and their feud.

Exam focus

How can I write about Shakespeare's use of imagery? AO2

You can use a particular image and consider how Shakespeare uses it to add layers to the meaning.

> Shakespeare uses images of light and the heavens to symbolise how bright and pure Romeo's love for Juliet really is. He describes her in heavenly terms, describing her eyes as 'Two of the fairest stars in all the heavens'. By choosing the idea of stars against the night sky, Shakespeare reminds us that their love is often connected to night time, and to secrecy. In this way the love of Romeo and Juliet can be seen as symbolic, like a gentle light trying to break through the 'darkness' of the family feud.

- A clear statement about what Shakespeare is doing
- An apt quotation well embedded
- Comment on this use of imagery and its meaning

Now you try!

Finish this paragraph about another image used by Shakespeare in the play. Try to explain how it adds to the meaning. Use one of the quotations from the list above.

Shakespeare presents the Friar as a knowledgeable man when ....

My progress   Needs more work ☐   Getting there ☐   Sorted! ☐

59

LANGUAGE Dramatic techniques

Five key things about Shakespeare's use of dramatic techniques

1. Shakespeare raises the **tension** in the play through moments of **dramatic irony**.
2. Shakespeare uses **soliloquy** to give an **insight into a character's innermost thoughts** and genuine feelings.
3. Soliloquy can also be used to **introduce characters**.
4. Shakespeare uses **foreshadowing** as a means of **building tension** throughout the play.
5. Foreshadowing and dramatic irony **impress on an audience** that we are **powerless** to stop the **tragedy** unfolding.

How does Shakespeare use dramatic irony?

- Shakespeare uses dramatic irony at the feast, where Juliet is meant to **'look to like'** Paris, but instead ends up liking the look of Romeo.
- Dramatic irony is created in a highly tense way when Romeo becomes the **'fortune's fool'** who kills Tybalt and faces banishment even though he has tried to avoid the violence in the streets.

How does Shakespeare use foreshadowing in the play?

- Shakespeare uses foreshadowing to reveal Romeo's ill-feeling about the **'consequence'** of the Capulet feast.
- Both lovers have a sense of danger when Romeo is in the orchard and when he leaves after their wedding night.
- Shakespeare foreshadows the tragic ending of the play when Juliet questions the wisdom of taking the Friar's potion, which she fears may be **'poison'**.

How does Shakespeare use soliloquy in the play?

- A soliloquy introduces the character of Friar Lawrence and his skills in making potions and medicines.
- Soliloquy is used to dramatic effect when Juliet waits for Romeo to arrive for their wedding night. Her hopeful thoughts contrast with the violence of Mercutio and Tybalt's deaths in the previous scene.
- Shakespeare reinforces Juliet's isolation in her later soliloquy when she is about to take the potion. Here her thoughts are panic-stricken and fearful.

LANGUAGE Dramatic techniques

Five key quotations

1. An invitation to the feast: **'My master is the great rich Capulet, and if you not be of the house of Montagues, I pray come and crush a cup of wine'** (I.2.80–2)
2. Juliet's concerns: **'It is too rash, too unadvis'd, too sudden,/Too like the lightning'** (II.2.118–19)
3. Romeo: **'More light and light, more dark and dark our woes!'** (III.5.36)
4. Juliet: **'Methinks I see thee now, thou art so low,/As one dead in the bottom of a tomb'** (III.5.55–6)
5. Juliet, before taking the potion: **'I have a faint cold fear thrills through my veins/That almost freezes up the heat of life'** (IV.3.15–16)

Note it!

Note how Shakespeare uses dramatic techniques to create moments of light and shade. For example, moments of high dramatic irony such as Mercutio and Tybalt's death are juxtaposed with Juliet's thoughtful soliloquy.

Exam focus

How can I write about Shakespeare's use of dramatic techniques? (AO2)

You can write about the effect of one dramatic technique.

> Shakespeare creates a feeling of anticipation right through the play. From the moment the servant unwittingly invites the Montagues to the feast to 'come and crush a cup of wine'. We know that Shakespeare is setting up a situation that will place the future lovers together. The dramatic irony is clear to the audience as we know that Capulet is hoping to bring Paris and Juliet together at the feast.

- Considers an effect
- Pinpoints a precise moment in the play
- Identifies Shakespeare's method and explains

Now you try!

Choose a different method used by Shakespeare and explain why he uses it and its possible impact. Use one of the quotations from the list above.

Shakespeare uses foreshadowing when Juliet imagines Romeo ....

My progress   Needs more work ☐   Getting there ☐   Sorted! ☐

EXAM PRACTICE Understanding the exam

Five key things about the exam

1. You will have **one** question on *Romeo and Juliet* which will be based on a **passage** given to you on the exam paper.
2. It will focus on **Shakespeare's presentation** of an aspect of the play, such as a **character**, **relationship** or a **theme**.
3. You will have about **45–50 minutes** to read and respond to the question.
4. The question is worth **30 marks**.
5. The question assesses **AOs 1, 2, 3, with an extra 4 marks for AO4**. Remember that **AO3** relates to **context**.

What will a question look like?

1. Starting with this extract, explore how Shakespeare presents Tybalt as aggressive.

Write about:
- how Shakespeare presents Tybalt as aggressive in this extract
- how Shakespeare presents Tybalt as aggressive in the play as a whole.

[30 marks] AO4 [4 marks]

- You must refer to the given passage
- You must explain the techniques Shakespeare uses
- This is the area you must tackle
- A reminder to begin with the given extract
- A reminder to **also** write about the whole of the play

Do all questions look the same?

- Not all questions will begin this way. Some might contain statements you must argue for or against. For example, **'Shakespeare's presentation of Verona shows it to be male-dominated.' Starting with this extract, explore how far you agree with this opinion.**
- Not all questions are about a single character. Some might ask you about a **relationship** between two characters, e.g. between Capulet and his wife.

EXAM PRACTICE The exam

What do I need to do to get a good mark?

Use this grid to understand what your current level is and how to improve it:

	AO1 Read, understand, respond	**AO2** Analyse language, form, structure and effects	**AO3** Show understanding of contexts
High	• You make **precise references** to the **passage** and *Romeo and Juliet* **as a whole**. • Your argument is **well-structured**, with quotations **fluently embedded** in sentences. • You cover **both** the extract and the whole play.	• You **analyse** and **interpret** the methods Shakespeare uses **very effectively**. • You **explore thoughtfully** the effects of these on the reader. • You show **excellent use** of subject terminology.	• You make **detailed, relevant links** between specific elements of the play and social and historical contexts.
Mid	• You make a **range of references** to the passage and the play as a whole. • You respond in **a clear, logical way** with **relevant** quotations chosen.	• You **explain clearly** some of the methods Shakespeare uses, and **some effects** on the reader. • You use **mostly relevant** subject terminology.	• You show **clear evidence** of understanding context which is **linked** to the play in places.
Lower	• You make **some references** to the passage and play as a whole, but in rather a **patchy** way. • You make **some useful points** but evidence is **not always clear or relevant**.	• You make **occasional attempts** to explain Shakespeare's methods but these are a little **unclear**. • You show **some use** of subject terminology.	• You demonstrate **basic awareness** of context but **links** to the play are **undeveloped** and **not always relevant**.

AO4 You can gain up to 4 marks for **AO4**, which assesses your use of spelling, punctuation and grammar. For top marks: use a **range** of vocabulary and sentence structures, adopt a **clear, purposeful and effective** writing style, and make sure your spelling and punctuation are **accurate**.

EXAM PRACTICE Character questions

Read these exam-style character questions

Read the following extract from Act II Scene II of *Romeo and Juliet* and then answer the question that follows.

At this point in the play Juliet speaks to Romeo in the orchard after the feast.

	JULIET	Thou knowest the mask of night is on my face,
		Else would a maiden blush bepaint my cheek
		For that which thou hast heard me speak tonight.
		Fain would I dwell on form, fain, fain deny
5		What I have spoke, but farewell compliment.
		Dost thou love me? I know thou wilt say 'Ay';
		And I will take thy word; yet if thou swear'st,
		Thou mayst prove false: at lovers' perjuries
		They say Jove laughs. O gentle Romeo,
10		If thou dost love, pronounce it faithfully;
		Or if thou think'st I am too quickly won,
		I'll frown and be perverse, and say thee nay,
		So thou wilt woo, but else not for the world.
		In truth, fair Montague, I am too fond,
15		And therefore thou mayst think my behaviour light:
		But trust me, gentleman, I'll prove more true
		Than those that have more coying to be strange.
		I should have been more strange, I must confess,
		But that thou overheard'st, ere I was ware,
20		My true-love passion; therefore pardon me,
		And not impute this yielding to light love,
		Which the dark night hath so discovered.
	ROMEO	Lady, by yonder blessed moon I vow,
		That tips with silver all these fruit-tree tops—
25	JULIET	O swear not by the moon, th'inconstant moon,
		That monthly changes in her circled orb,
		Lest that thy love prove likewise variable.

2. Starting with this moment in the play, explore how Shakespeare presents Juliet as being honest and loyal. Write about:
- how Shakespeare presents Juliet as honest and loyal in this extract
- how Juliet is presented as honest and loyal in the play as a whole.

[30 marks] AO4 [4 marks]

EXAM PRACTICE Character questions

Read this passage from Act II Scene III of *Romeo and Juliet*.
Romeo has told Friar Lawrence he loves Juliet and asks him to marry them.

	FRIAR LAWRENCE	Holy Saint Francis, what a change is here!
		Is Rosaline, that thou didst love so dear,
		So soon forsaken? Young men's love then lies
		Not truly in their hearts, but in their eyes.
5		Jesu Maria, what a deal of brine
		Hath wash'd thy sallow cheeks for Rosaline!
		How much salt water thrown away in waste,
		To season love, that of it doth not taste!
		The sun not yet thy sighs from heaven clears,
10		Thy old groans yet ringing in my ancient ears;
		Lo here upon thy cheek the stain doth sit
		Of an old tear that is not wash'd off yet.
		If e'er thou wast thyself, and these woes thine,
		Thou and these woes were all for Rosaline.
		And art thou chang'd? Pronounce this sentence then:
15		Women may fall, when there's no strength in men.
	ROMEO	Thou chid'st me oft for loving Rosaline.
	FRIAR LAWRENCE	For doting, not for loving, pupil mine.
	ROMEO	And bad'st me bury love.
	FRIAR LAWRENCE	Not in a grave,
20		To lay one in, another out to have.
	ROMEO	I pray thee chide me not. Her I love now
		Doth grace for grace and love for love allow;
		The other did not so.
	FRIAR LAWRENCE	O she knew well
25		Thy love did read by rote, that could not spell.
		But come, young waverer, come go with me,
		In one respect I'll thy assistant be:
		For this alliance may so happy prove
		To turn your households' rancour to pure love.
	ROMEO	O let us hence, I stand on sudden haste.
	FRIAR LAWRENCE	Wisely and slow, they stumble that run fast.

3. 'Shakespeare presents Friar Lawrence as a good adviser to Romeo.'
Explore how far you agree with this statement. Write about:
- how Friar Lawrence is presented as a good adviser in this extract
- how Friar Lawrence is presented as a good adviser in the play as a whole.

[30 marks] AO4 [4 marks]

EXAM PRACTICE Planning your character response

Five key stages to follow

1. **Read** the **question**; **highlight** the key words.
2. **Read** the **extract** with the **key words** from the **question** in mind.
3. Quickly **generate ideas** for your response.
4. **Plan** for paragraphs.
5. **Write** your response; **check it** against your plan as you progress.

What do I focus on?

Highlight the **key words**:

> 2. Starting with this moment in the play, explore how Shakespeare presents Juliet as being honest and loyal. Write about:
> - how Shakespeare presents Juliet as honest and loyal in this extract
> - how Juliet is presented as honest and loyal in the play as a whole.

What do they tell you? Focus on both extract and the whole text; explain Shakespeare's methods; stick to Juliet's honesty and loyalty as the topic.

How should I read the passage?

- Check for any immediate links to the question (e.g. Juliet is honest about her feelings, knowing Romeo overheard her speaking them aloud).
- Look for any evidence/quotations you could highlight (e.g. **'Fain would I dwell on form, fain, fain deny/ What I have spoke'**).

How do I get my ideas?

Note your ideas in a spider diagram or list them in a table:

The extract

Juliet is honest and open; asks for Romeo's forgiveness for her boldness

Promises to be true to Romeo; asks for the same in return from Romeo

Juliet's honesty and loyalty

The play as a whole

Juliet maintains her loyalty to Romeo after Tybalt has been killed

She is dishonest with her parents when she agrees to marry Paris

EXAM PRACTICE Planning your character response

The extract	The play as a whole
• Juliet doesn't deny what Romeo overheard in the orchard • Asks Romeo's forgiveness for seeming to be too bold	• Juliet is shocked by Tybalt's death, but remains loyal to Romeo • Is faithful to Romeo but dishonest with her parents

How do I structure my ideas?

Make a **plan** for **paragraphs**.* Decide the order for your points:

- Paragraph 1: Go straight into your first point: *In the extract Juliet is embarrassed at being overheard, 'a maiden blush', but doesn't deny her feelings. At the feast, she'd decided that Romeo would be her 'only love'.*
- Paragraph 2: *Juliet shows her readiness to be loyal to Romeo, 'I'll prove more true'; asks in return, 'pronounce it faithfully'. Genuine, as later they marry.*
- Paragraph 3: *Juliet worries Romeo will think she is 'too quickly won'; says she could tease him and pretend otherwise. Elsewhere, shows she can pretend well when she is dishonest with her parents and Nurse.*
- Paragraph 4: *Mention of the 'inconstant moon'; wants him to be loyal and suggests she will be too. Dramatic irony of their relationship being hidden.*
- Paragraph 5: *Juliet says her love is not a 'light love' compared to the 'dark night'. Later she will face the darkness of the tomb to be reunited with him.*

How do I write effectively?

Write **clear**, **analytical** paragraphs and **embed** your evidence. For example:

> In the extract, Shakespeare shows us how Juliet is embarrassed at being overheard confessing her love for Romeo and suggests he would see her 'maiden blush' if it were light. She is honest with Romeo and does not deny her feelings despite her tone of modesty and shyness. Earlier at the feast we saw her making a clear decision that Romeo would be her 'only love' despite being 'sprung from my only hate' and she reinforces this loyalty to him here.

- Overview point – extract
- Key term
- Link to rest of play
- Quotations embedded in the sentence
- Summary point

Now you try!

Re-read Question 3 on page 65 and plan your response in the same way.

* The plan above and the sample answers on pages 68 and 70 have five paragraphs, but you don't need to be limited to this if you have more points to include.

EXAM PRACTICE Grade 5 annotated sample answer

What does a Grade 5 answer look like?

Read the task again, then the sample answer below.

> **2.** Starting with this moment in the play, explore how Shakespeare presents Juliet as being honest and loyal. Write about:
> - how Shakespeare presents Juliet as honest and loyal in this extract
> - how Juliet is presented as honest and loyal in the play as a whole.
>
> **[30 marks] AO4 [4 marks]**

In this extract Juliet is really embarrassed about Romeo overhearing her and glad it is dark so Romeo can't see her blushing. We know this when she says 'a maiden blush bepaint my cheek', However, she is upfront and honest with Romeo and doesn't hide her feelings. She stands by what she said showing she is loyal to him. Earlier at the feast we see she is going to be loyal to Romeo even though he is a Montague. She says 'my only love sprung from my only hate' suggesting she is going to put him first.

Juliet tells Romeo that she is not like other girls he might have met and she will 'prove more true than those that have more coying to be strange'. Because Juliet is loyal she wants Romeo to be loyal as well and uses questions such as 'Dost thou love me?'. This shows us she wants a relationship based on honesty. This seems to show they are serious and really in love. We see later in the play Juliet makes a serious loyal commitment and marries Romeo at the Friar's cell.

Juliet is worried that Romeo thinks she is not behaving like a young woman should. She jokes she could pretend not to be, 'I'll frown and be perverse'. This could be a different side to Juliet though. We can see she is quite a good actress as later on she convinces the Nurse and her parents that she will marry Paris. This shows us she has a dishonest side to her as well.

Annotations:
- **AO1** Establishes a clear point about plot with support
- **AO4** Informal language
- **AO1** Makes a clear link to elsewhere in the play
- **AO2** Identifies a useful reference but could analyse this language feature more closely
- **AO2** Identifies another feature but does not analyse fully
- **AO3** Weak point about social context
- **AO1** Makes contrasting point but could embed quotation more fluently
- **AO1** Links to another part of the play but could interpret more fully

EXAM PRACTICE Grade 5 annotated sample answer

> Juliet seems to want to feel secure in her relationship. She tells Romeo not to swear on the 'inconstant moon'. This personifies the moon as something unfaithful and always changing. She wants Romeo to be loyal to her which suggests she would be loyal back. However, a lot of the time Shakespeare links their love to the moon and the stars. Later in the play Juliet thinks about Romeo being 'cut out in little stars' when she waits for him on their wedding night.
>
> In the extract Juliet says her love is honest and loyal and not a 'light love', meaning one which is not serious. She mentions Romeo has discovered it on a 'dark night'. This implies that although Juliet was honest and loyal to Romeo she was deceiving her family, which would be very serious at the time as society was very strict on daughters. A lot of the time her love was a secret and happened at night. At the end of the play, Juliet is still loyal to Romeo but she is in the dark and frightening tomb. Shakespeare uses light and dark to show the two sides to Juliet.

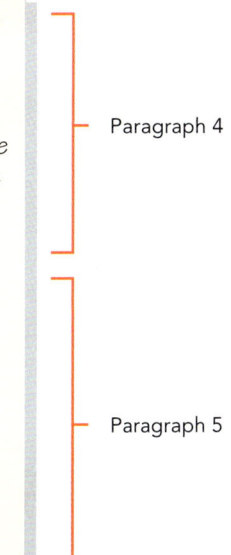

— Paragraph 4

— Paragraph 5

Check the skills

Re-read paragraphs four and five of this response and:
- highlight other **points** made;
- circle any reference to **context**;
- underline any places where the student has made an **interpretation**.

Now you try!

Look again at paragraph three (*'We can see Juliet is quite worried ...'* etc.) and improve it by:
- Adding a **reference or quotation** to show how she deceives the Nurse or her parents.
- **Explaining** the effect of Shakespeare's use of **contrast** when he presents Juliet.
- Ending with a more detailed **summary point** about her dishonest side.
- Improving the overall **style** by making sure you express yourself in a formal way; using **connectives** to **link** ideas.

69

EXAM PRACTICE Grade 7+ annotated sample answer

What does a Grade 7+ answer look like?

Read the task again, then the sample answer below.

> 2. Starting with this moment in the play, explore how Shakespeare presents Juliet as being honest and loyal. Write about:
> - how Shakespeare presents Juliet as honest and loyal in this extract
> - how Juliet is presented as honest and loyal in the play as a whole.
>
> [30 marks] AO4 [4 marks]

Juliet is presented as modest and open in the extract where she is glad of the 'mask of night' to hide the 'maiden blush' in her cheeks, suggesting that she was not expecting her feelings for Romeo to be overheard. Despite her innocence and demure nature she shows a sense of honesty and genuine love when she confirms her feelings. Her repetition of 'Fain, fain deny' reinforce her honesty to Romeo about her love for him from the start.

Juliet also demonstrates her desire to be loyal to Romeo by asking for those same qualities to be returned. She questions him directly, 'Dost thou love me?' which implies she wants no secrets between them and that she is serious about this love. Later in the scene, she questions Romeo again as to whether his 'purpose [is] marriage', suggesting she expects a commitment from Romeo in return for her own pledge of loyalty. We witness their loyalty to each other when they do marry later in the play at Friar Lawrence's cell.

However, this loyalty to Romeo masks dishonesty with regard to her parents. Juliet is aware they are planning her marriage to Paris. We might question whether Juliet's motives for marrying Romeo so quickly are to ensure she marries the man of her choice; not her father's. This seems to cause Juliet some anxiety as she worries that Romeo might find her 'too quickly won'. Juliet contradicts the expected 'compliment' of the time for daughters of wealthy households. It could be said that she is actively disloyal to her father who later labels her a 'disobedient wretch!'

AO1 A clear statement opening the argument with subtle use of embedded textual details

AO2 A linguistic point identified with a comment linked to the task

AO2 A further method identified and explored in detail with a link showing detailed knowledge of the play

AO1 Makes a seamless link and connection to the counter argument

AO4 A well expressed complex sentence

AO3 Shows perceptive contextual knowledge and blends this fluently into the response

EXAM PRACTICE Grade 7+ annotated sample answer

> Shakespeare uses many images connected with the heavens in presenting Romeo and Juliet's love. For example, earlier in the play we see Romeo refer to Juliet positively using the metaphor 'a bright angel'. However, here Juliet sees 'th'inconstant moon' as a negative image, believing it to be too changeable and not representative of the loyalty she displays and expects. This is somewhat ironic as much of the lovers' relationship has to be hidden from others or takes place under the 'mask of night'. — Paragraph 4
>
> Despite this secrecy, Juliet remains loyal to Romeo and demonstrates that hers is a 'true-love passion' and not 'light love'. She defends Romeo through the darkest moments, placing her 'only love' above the family's 'only hate' for the Montagues. This is especially clear following Tybalt's death. Juliet places herself in danger to escape marriage to Paris and experiences a further 'dark night' in the Capulet tomb. However, there is an inherent contradiction in Shakespeare's presentation of her. Ironically, although he portrays Juliet's clear dishonesty towards her parents and trusted Nurse, she is remembered as 'Romeo's faithful wife' once dead. — Paragraph 5

Check the skills

Re-read paragraphs four and five of this response and:
- identify any particularly **fluent** or **well-expressed** ideas;
- find any further references to **Shakespeare's language and techniques**;
- highlight any places where the student has shown **deeper insight** and offered **original** or particularly **thoughtful** ideas or made interesting **links**.

Now you try!

Now, using the plan you made for Question 3 on page 67, write a full response. Here's a reminder of the question:

3. 'Shakespeare's presentation of Friar Lawrence suggests he is a good adviser to Romeo.' Starting with this extract, explore how far you agree with this statement. Write about:
- how Friar Lawrence is presented as a good adviser in this extract
- how he is presented as a good adviser in the play as a whole.

[30 marks] AO4 [4 marks]

- Try to match your answer to the High Level objectives on page 63.

EXAM PRACTICE Theme questions

Read these exam-style theme questions

Read the following extract from Act III Scene 5 of *Romeo and Juliet* and then answer the question that follows.

At this point in the play Romeo is saying goodbye to Juliet after their wedding night.

	ROMEO	Farewell, farewell! one kiss, and I'll descend.
	[He goeth down]	
	JULIET	Art thou gone so, love, lord, ay, husband, friend?
		I must hear from thee every day in the hour,
5		For in a minute there are many days.
		O, by this count I shall be much in years
		Ere I again behold my Romeo!
	ROMEO	Farewell!
	[From below]	I will omit no opportunity
10		That may convey my greetings, love, to thee.
	JULIET	O think'st thou we shall ever meet again?
	ROMEO	I doubt it not, and all these woes shall serve
		For sweet discourses in our times to come.
	JULIET	O God, I have an ill-divining soul!
15		Methinks I see thee now, thou art so low,
		As one dead in the bottom of a tomb.
		Either my eyesight fails, or thou look'st pale.
	ROMEO	And trust me, love, in my eye so do you:
		Dry sorrow drinks our blood. Adieu, adieu!
20	*[Exit]*	
	JULIET	O Fortune, Fortune, all men call thee fickle;
		If thou art fickle, what dost thou with him
		That is renown'd for faith? Be fickle, Fortune:
		For then I hope thou wilt not keep him long,
25		But send him back.

4. Starting with this conversation, explore how Shakespeare presents ideas about fate and free will in *Romeo and Juliet*. Write about:
   - how Shakespeare presents fate and free will in this extract
   - how Shakespeare presents fate and free will in the play as a whole.

[30 marks] AO4 [4 marks]

EXAM PRACTICE Theme questions

Read the following extract from Act III Scene 2 of *Romeo and Juliet* and then answer the question that follows.

At this point in the play Juliet is waiting for Romeo following their wedding.

	JULIET	
	[…]	Spread thy close curtain, love-performing Night,
		That runaways' eyes may wink, and Romeo
		Leap to these arms, untalk'd of and unseen:
5		Lovers can see to do their amorous rites
		By their own beauties, or if love be blind,
		It best agrees with night. Come, civil Night,
		Thou sober-suited matron all in black,
		And learn me how to lose a winning match,
10		Play'd for a pair of stainless maidenhoods.
		Hood my unmann'd blood, bating in my cheeks,
		With thy black mantle, till strange love grow bold,
		Think true love acted simple modesty.
		Come, Night, come, Romeo, come, thou day in night,
15		For thou wilt lie upon the wings of night,
		Whiter than new snow upon a raven's back.
		Come, gentle Night, come, loving, black-brow'd Night,
		Give me my Romeo, and when I shall die,
		Take him and cut him out in little stars,
20		And he will make the face of heaven so fine
		That all the world will be in love with night,
		And pay no worship to the garish sun.
		O, I have bought the mansion of a love,
		But not possess'd it, and though I am sold,
25		Not yet enjoy'd.

5. Starting with this extract, explore how Shakespeare presents young love in *Romeo and Juliet*. Write about:
- how Shakespeare presents young love in this soliloquy
- how Shakespeare presents young love in the play as a whole.

[30 marks] AO4 [4 marks]

EXAM PRACTICE Planning your theme response

Five key stages to follow

1. **Read** the **question**; **highlight** key words.
2. **Read** the **extract** with the **key words** from the **question** in mind.
3. Quickly **generate ideas** for your response.
4. **Plan** for paragraphs.
5. **Write** your response; **check it** against your plan as you progress.

What do I focus on?

Highlight the **key words**:

4. Starting with this conversation, explore how Shakespeare presents ideas about fate and free will in *Romeo and Juliet*. Write about:
   - how Shakespeare presents fate and free will in this extract
   - how Shakespeare presents fate and free will in the play as a whole.

What do they tell you? Focus on both extract and whole text; explain what specific methods Shakespeare uses; stick to fate and free will as the main topic.

How should I read the passage?

- Check for any immediate links to the question (e.g. Romeo and Juliet have spent the night together as an act of free will despite Romeo's banishment).
- Look for any evidence/quotations you could highlight (e.g. **'I have an ill-divining soul!'**).

How do I get my ideas?

Note your ideas in a spider diagram or list them in a table:

The extract

Juliet wonders if she will see Romeo again – 'O think'st thou we shall ever meet again?'

Her words foreshadow the tragedy to come, 'Methinks I see thee now, thou art so low, As one dead in the bottom of a tomb.'

Fate and free will

The play as a whole

Romeo has an bad feeling about the Capulet feast

He feels he is 'fortune's fool' for avenging Mercutio's death

EXAM PRACTICE: Planning your theme response

The extract	The play as a whole
• Romeo suggests 'free will' will enable them to be together again, 'all these woes shall serve for sweet discourses in our times to come' • Juliet feels they are at fate's mercy, 'Fortune, all men call thee fickle'	• The Prologue suggests Romeo and Juliet were at the mercy of fate, 'star-cross'd' • Fate seems to work against the lovers, i.e. when Romeo, against his will, fights Tybalt

How do I structure my ideas?

Make a **plan** for **paragraphs**.* Decide the order for your points:

- Paragraph 1: Go straight into your first point: *In the extract Romeo and Juliet say goodbye – paying the price for their secret marriage/act of free will?*
- Paragraph 2: *Romeo more certain – feels their future is based on free will. Juliet feels a sense of foreboding. Contrasts with Romeo before the feast.*
- Paragraph 3: *In the extract the reference to the tomb suggests death and the tragedy to come, linking to Prologue/Shakespeare's dramatic tension.*
- Paragraph 4: *Reference to 'fortune' – Juliet calls on it for help. Contrasts with Romeo after Tybalt's death, 'fortune's fool'.*
- Paragraph 5: *Throughout, Shakespeare's use of structure has juxtaposed acts of free will with cruel twists of fate. Extract ends with Lady Capulet's entrance and the dramatic irony of her news.*

How do I write effectively?

Write **clear**, **analytical** paragraphs and **embed** your evidence. For example:

> In the extract, Romeo and Juliet are parting following their wedding night. Romeo asks for 'one kiss' which may be seen as symbolic of the one night they have been able to spend together. The many references to time in the extract suggest their time together has been cut short by Fate. This contrasts with earlier in the play when Juliet waited since 'The clock struck nine' to hear if Romeo has arranged for them to marry.

- Overview of extract
- Key term
- Link to rest of play
- Quotations embedded in the sentence

Now you try!

Re-read Question 5 on page 73 and plan your response in the same way.

* The plan above and the sample answers on pages 76 and 78 have five paragraphs, but you don't need to be limited to this if you have more points to include.

EXAM PRACTICE Grade 5 annotated sample answer

What does a Grade 5 answer look like?

Read the task again, then the sample answer below.

> 4. Starting with this conversation, explore how Shakespeare presents ideas about fate and free will in *Romeo and Juliet*. Write about:
>   - how Shakespeare presents fate and free will in this extract
>   - how Shakespeare presents fate and free will in the play as a whole.
>
>   [30 marks] AO4 [4 marks]

In the extract Romeo is about to leave Juliet after their wedding night. Romeo and Juliet have got married of their own free will but now it seems like fate has driven them apart. Romeo is in danger if he is found so leaves asking for 'one kiss'. Juliet is worried she might not see him again and asks a lot of questions, 'Art thou gone so, love…?'. This links to the night they met when Romeo was in the orchard. He was in danger there too and Juliet questioned if he loved her enough to marry her.

In the extract Romeo is acting like the stronger one even though he is in danger. He tries to reassure Juliet by saying, 'I doubt it not' and tries to say they have a future. Juliet is the one who is more worried and say she has 'an ill-divining soul' which means she has got a bad feeling. This reminds us of Romeo before the feast who felt that no good could come of going. In some ways he was right as his relationship has placed him in danger.

There are a lot of predictions like this in the play and Juliet goes on to compare Romeo climbing down from her room as if he is in a grave, 'As one dead in the bottom of a tomb.' This is a really grim prediction of when the two of them actually see each other again at the end of the play. This is another example of foreshadowing.

AO1 Makes a clear statement to set up a viewpoint and attempts an interpretation

AO2 Identifies an aspect of language with an example but does not explore the effect

AO1 Makes a link to another part of the play but does not link precisely to the question

AO1 Makes a valid point with support but interprets in a very basic way

AO4 This sentence is expressed rather informally

AO2 Identifies another aspect of Shakespeare's method but should embed the quotation fully and could be more precise and analytical

AO4 A rather clumsy end to the paragraph

EXAM PRACTICE Grade 5 annotated sample answer

Because the couple acted of their own free will and went against their society and families, it seems like they have brought a lot of bad luck on themselves. Juliet uses personification and tries to ask fate or fortune for help in the extract. She says, 'Be fickle, Fortune;' and asks fortune to change its mind and 'send him back' meaning, return Romeo to her. In the past fortune was not kind to Romeo as when he killed Tybalt he said he was 'fortune's fool'. — Paragraph 4

At the end of this extract, it becomes very dramatic because Romeo has only just left when Lady Capulet comes in to tell Juliet she is getting married to Paris. Shakespeare uses dramatic irony here as we the audience know what news she is bringing but Juliet doesn't. This seems like fate is being cruel. It's like it is a punishment for Romeo and Juliet being too free-willed and marrying in secret. — Paragraph 5

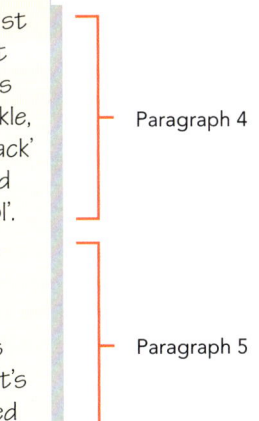

Check the skills

Re-read paragraphs four and five of this response and:
- highlight other **points** made;
- circle any reference to **context**;
- underline any places where the student has made an **interpretation**.

Now you try!

Look again at paragraph three ('*There are a lot of predictions …*' etc.) and improve it by:
- **Explaining** why the quotation from the extract referring to the tomb is important by interpreting it more analytically.
- Adding a **reference or quotation** which shows the link with the final scene and explains it.
- Ending with a **summary point** about foreshadowing which is fully explained and considers the effect Shakespeare creates.
- Improving the overall **style** by making sure your sentences **flow**; using **connectives** to **link** ideas.

77

EXAM PRACTICE Grade 7+ annotated sample answer

What does a Grade 7+ answer look like?

Read the task again, then the sample answer below.

> 4. Starting with this conversation, explore how Shakespeare presents ideas about fate and free will in *Romeo and Juliet*. Write about:
>   - how Shakespeare presents fate and free will in this extract
>   - how Shakespeare presents fate and free will in the play as a whole.
>
> [30 marks] AO4 [4 marks]

This poignant extract shows Romeo and Juliet parting after their one night together. Romeo reinforces this by asking for 'one kiss' which seems to symbolise the short time they have spent together. Shakespeare peppers the extract with many references to time, 'every day', 'the hour', 'in a minute', which reinforces the speed of their relationship and also suggests that they are operating against wider forces beyond their control – the stars, the heavens and Fate itself. Their awareness of the swift passing of time contrasts with how 'much in years' Juliet feels she may have to wait for Romeo and his thoughts on 'times to come'. Such references remind us of Friar Lawrence's warning about the speed with which they married of their own freewill, 'Wisely and slow, they stumble that run fast' and it seems that now the couple are facing dire consequences for their earlier haste.

Those consequences are emphasised by Juliet's sense of foreboding as she describes her 'ill-divining soul'. This echoes Romeo's feelings before he met Juliet at the Capulet feast when he sensed 'Some consequence yet hanging in the stars'. In this way Shakespeare imbues both their meeting and their parting with a sense of fate from which neither can escape.

Indeed, their future fates are almost spelt out for us when Juliet likens Romeo's descent from her room to being 'dead in the bottom of a tomb'. Shakespeare heightens the dramatic tension here, making connections with the start of the play when we learned in the Prologue that the couple had a 'death-mark'd love'. We experience a grim foreshadowing of the moment when the lovers are indeed reunited in the Capulet tomb.

Annotations:

- **AO1** Makes a confident start with an interpretation of the plot
- **AO2** Identifies writer's method and selects some well-chosen textual details
- **AO1** Makes a very appropriate link to another part of the play
- **AO4** Uses sophisticated vocabulary and grammatical structures to express ideas
- **AO2** Confidently explores writer's method and shows a wide ranging knowledge of the play

78

EXAM PRACTICE Grade 7+ annotated sample answer

> Yet, the lovers have acted out of free will in defying the conventions of their society, placing themselves in danger and potentially jeopardising the honour of both of their families. However, Romeo and Juliet share a belief that it is fate that has ensnared them and could be their salvation. In the extract Juliet appeals to the fickle nature of a personified fortune to release Romeo and 'send him back'. This is somewhat ironic in that Romeo felt he was 'fortune's fool' when he killed Tybalt. It suggests the lovers are merely the playthings of a higher power. — Paragraph 4
>
> To emphasise this, Shakespeare juxtaposes every act of free will the lovers make with apparently cruel twists of fate. We see this most clearly when Juliet is drawn to Romeo at the feast rather than to Paris; when Romeo is led to avenge Mercutio's death so soon after his wedding and when Friar Lawrence is unable to communicate his plans to Romeo at the end of the play. The extract culminates with the departure of Romeo. The dramatic irony is clear: as one wedding day ends, another is about to be announced. Lady Capulet's news leads Juliet to engage in her final tragic act of free will and Romeo to choose to 'defy' the stars, defy fate itself and choose his own tragic demise. — Paragraph 5

Check the skills

Re-read paragraphs four and five of this response and:
- highlight any particularly **fluent** or **well-expressed** ideas;
- circle any references to **context**;
- underline places where the student has shown **deeper insight** and offered **original** or particularly **thoughtful** ideas or made interesting **links**.

Now you try!

Now, using the plan you made for Question 5 on page 75, write a full response. Here's a reminder of the question:

5. Starting with this extract, explore how Shakespeare presents young love in Romeo and Juliet. Write about:
- how Shakespeare presents young love in this soliloquy
- how Shakespeare presents young love in the play as a whole.

[30 marks] AO4 [4 marks]

- Try to match your answer to the High Level objectives on page 63.

EXAM PRACTICE Practice questions

Now you try!

Now, apply the skills you have learned to these two new questions:
- Note down key points from the extract.
- Select the key quotations you want to use from the extract.
- Repeat the process with other ideas from the play as a whole.
- Write your answer.
- Look at the suggested list of key points in the **Answers** (page 88).

Read this extract from Act III Scene 5 of *Romeo and Juliet* and then answer the question that follows.

At this point in the play Lady Capulet gives Juliet the news of her arranged marriage.

	LADY CAPULET	Marry, my child, early next Thursday morn,
		The gallant, young, and noble gentleman,
		The County Paris, at Saint Peter's Church,
		Shall happily make thee there a joyful bride.
5	JULIET	Now by Saint Peter's Church and Peter too,
		He shall not make me there a joyful bride.
		I wonder at this haste, that I must wed
		Ere he that should be husband comes to woo.
		I pray you tell my lord and father, madam,
10		I will not marry yet, and when I do, I swear
		It shall be Romeo, whom you know I hate,
		Rather than Paris. These are news indeed!
	LADY CAPULET	Here comes your father, tell him so yourself;
		And see how he will take it at your hands.

6. Starting with this conversation, explore how Shakespeare presents the relationship between Juliet and her mother. Write about:
   - how Shakespeare presents the relationship between Juliet and her mother in this extract
   - how Shakespeare presents the relationship between Juliet and her mother in the play as a whole.

[30 marks] AO4 [4 marks]

EXAM PRACTICE *Practice questions*

Read the following extract from Act III Scene 4 of *Romeo and Juliet* and then answer the question that follows:

In this scene Capulet arranges Juliet's marriage to Paris.

	CAPULET	Sir Paris, I will make a desperate tender
		Of my child's love: I think she will be rul'd
		In all respects by me; nay more, I doubt it not.
		Wife, go you to her ere you go to bed,
5		Acquaint her here of my son Paris' love,
		And bid her—mark you me?—on Wednesday next—
		But soft, what day is this?
	PARIS	Monday my lord.
	CAPULET	Monday, ha, ha! Well, Wednesday is too soon,
10		A'Thursday let it be—a'Thursday, tell her,
		She shall be married to this noble earl.
		Will you be ready? do you like this haste?
		Well, keep no great ado—a friend or two,
		For hark you, Tybalt being slain so late,
15		It may be thought we held him carelessly,
		Being our kinsman, if we revel much:
		Therefore we'll have some half a dozen friends,
		And there an end. But what say you to Thursday?
	PARIS	My lord, I would that Thursday were tomorrow.
20	CAPULET	Well, get you gone, a'Thursday be it then.—
		Go you to Juliet ere you go to bed,
		Prepare her, wife, against this wedding day.
		Farewell, my lord. Light to my chamber, ho!
		Afore me, it is so very late that we
		May call it early by and by. Good night.

7. Starting with this conversation, explore how Shakespeare presents family power in *Romeo and Juliet*. Write about:
- how family power is presented in this extract
- how family power is presented in the play as a whole.

[30 marks] AO4 [4 marks]

GLOSSARY

Literary or language term	Explanation
blank verse	unrhymed iambic pentameter
climax	the high point of the action
connective	a link between paragraphs to show the relationship between them
contrast	something that creates an opposite effect, e.g. light and dark
courtly love	a tradition from medieval literature where a knight yearns for the love of a lady and the love is not returned
denouement	the ending of the play
dialogue	a conversation between two or more characters; the words spoken by a character
dramatic irony	when the audience knows more about what is happening than some of the characters
exposition	an introduction or opening
falling action	where the plot begins to take a downward turn or unravel
foreshadowing	a warning that something will follow later
imagery	descriptive language using visual images to make actions, objects and characters more vivid for the audience
irony	when someone deliberately says one thing when they mean another
juxtaposition	when two ideas or events are placed deliberately one after the other to create a dramatic effect
metaphor	when one thing is used to describe another thing to create an unusual or striking image
oxymoron	when contradictory terms are brought together
plot	the storyline
prose	lines of text with no rhyme
Renaissance	the period in history linked with a cultural 'rebirth'
rising action	a growth in the tension of the **plot**
simile	when one thing is compared directly to another using 'like' or 'as'
soliloquy	when a character speaks their thoughts, usually when alone on stage
structure	the shape or way a text is built, organised or put together
symbol	something that represents something else, usually with meanings that are widely known (e.g. a dove as a sign of peace)
theme	an idea that reoccurs through a text
tragedy	a drama dealing with tragic events

ANSWERS

Note that the sample paragraphs given here provide only one possible approach to each task. Many other approaches would also be valid and appropriate.

PLOT AND STRUCTURE

Act I Scene 1 – Now you try! (page 5)
Shakespeare presents the character of Benvolio as sensible to contrast with Tybalt. In the fight in Act I it is Benvolio who intervenes with his calming words, 'Put up your swords, you know not what you do.' This suggests that Benvolio is not as violent as some of the other young men and is keen to keep the peace as the Prince later commands.

Act I Scenes 2–5 – Now you try! (page 7)
Lady Capulet seems keen for Juliet to look positively at Paris and consider his proposal. She asks Juliet, 'How stands your disposition to be married?' in rather a blunt way and a way which is rather a shock and surprise to Juliet. However, at this time securing a good marriage was very important for a woman of fortune to secure her future. Perhaps Lady Capulet, whilst seeming cold, may have Juliet's best interests at heart.

Act II Scenes 1 and 2 – Now you try! (page 9)
Romeo also describes his love for Juliet as giving him wings so that he could fly to be with her. To access the orchard he has used, 'love's light wings' which creates an image of an angel or perhaps even Cupid who is connected with love.

Act II Scenes 3–6 – Now you try! (page 11)
The Friar also seems genuinely concerned about Romeo and his happiness. Though he is shocked at Romeo's sudden change of heart from loving Rosaline, he does agree to help Romeo and to perform the marriage to Juliet. He does this with the best of intentions believing that 'this alliance may so happy prove/To turn your households' rancour to pure love.'

Act III Scenes 1 and 2 – Now you try! (page 13)
We see the impact of the fight when Mercutio collapses and curses both the Capulets and the Montagues with 'A plague a' both your houses!' At this moment it seems that Mercutio realises too late that his hasty actions in rising to Tybalt's challenge have cost him his life. It shows the tragic loss of young life that can occur as a result of the seemingly pointless feud and grimly foreshadows the even greater tragedy to come.

Act III Scenes 3–5 – Now you try! (page 15)
Juliet's mother reacts by rejecting her daughter's pleas for help and support. She coldly brushes Juliet aside and instructs Juliet: 'Talk not to me, for I'll not speak a word.' This could imply that her mother feels that Juliet will dishonour the Capulets by refusing to marry Paris, or it could suggest that she herself does not wish to anger Capulet by supporting Juliet. In either case, her cold response helps to leave Juliet isolated and with a stark choice.

Act IV – Now you try! (page 17)
Juliet is also presented as quite capable of deception when she pretends to be obedient to her parents' wishes. She begs of Capulet his 'Pardon' and suggests that, 'Henceforward I am ever rul'd by you.' Her acting here is convincing for Capulet; however, we as the audience realise that Juliet is planning to fake her own death. This helps to show us a very different side to Juliet – one that is determined to forge her own destiny and be with the man she loves and one who is not about to be 'rul'd' by her father.

Act V – Now you try! (page 19)
Romeo reacts strongly when he hears that Juliet is dead. Though he placed his trust in fate to bring them back together earlier in the play, here he openly challenges the heavens, 'I defy you, stars!' In this way, it seems that Romeo is determined to take charge of his own destiny and we are given a sense of what this might be when he visits the apothecary for poison before returning to Verona.

Form and structure – Now you try! (page 21)
However, Shakespeare also shows us that it is not just the young who can act hastily. Despite his earlier claim that Juliet is too young to marry, Capulet is swift to confirm the wedding to Paris following Tybalt's murder. He suggests, 'Monday, ha ha! Well, Wednesday is too soon', and instructs his wife, 'a' Thursday, tell her'. Perhaps Capulet is anxious that Paris will lose interest in a marriage to a Capulet after the brawl in the streets. However, his hasty decision will ultimately cost him his only daughter's life.

Quick revision – Quick quiz (pages 22–3)
1. Benvolio 2. Rosaline 3. Paris 4. From a servant delivering the invitations 5. Lady Capulet 6. Tybalt 7. The sun 8. Send a messenger to him 9. Friar Lawrence's cell 10. Juliet 11. Because it is hot and the Capulets will be out looking for trouble 12. Mercutio 13. 'a plague upon both your houses' 14. A ring 15. Thursday 16. Mantua 17. Paris 18. That the potion will not work; that it may be a poison 19. Friar John 20. Paris

Quick revision – Power paragraphs (page 23)
1. Mercutio's death provides a turning point in the play. It acts as the trigger for Romeo to seek revenge on Tybalt for the murder of his good friend, leading to him to realise too late that he is 'fortune's fool'. Mercutio's death and its consequences lead to Romeo's banishment and his separation from Juliet. The dream of reconciling the two houses of Montague and Capulet seems impossible at this moment in the play.

83

ANSWERS

2. On the surface, Friar Lawrence seems to be helpful to the two young lovers because he sees a possible positive outcome from their marriage in that it may 'turn your households' rancour to pure love'. However, he does not consider the consequences of marrying the young couple in secret and cannot foresee the problems this will cause. His actions lead to him offering more and more dangerous choices to both Romeo and Juliet and his failure to reach Romeo in time contributes to both of the young lovers taking their own lives.

Quick revision – Exam practice (page 23)
- In this soliloquy we can see Juliet's true feelings for Romeo. We are convinced that her love for him is genuine and passionate as she hopes that Romeo will soon 'leap to these arms, untalk'd of and unseen'. However, it also shows her reckless side as she does not consider the impact that their secret marriage is going to have or the danger Romeo would be in if he was found at Capulet's house.
- Juliet shows her love by comparing Romeo to the stars in the sky, suggesting that 'he will make the face of heaven so fine'. This creates an impression of Romeo's goodness and beauty in Juliet's eyes and mirrors the way he has described her earlier in the play. It seems to suggest that both of the lovers view each other as heavenly beings. However, the speech is also filled with images of the night. Juliet sees the night as 'gentle' and 'loving' but it also reinforces the secrecy of their relationship and the future darkness they will both face.

SETTING AND CONTEXT

Elizabethan society – Now you try! (page 25)
Shakespeare shows us how fearful Juliet is of the crypt, suggesting it may be haunted by Tybalt's ghost, 'Methinks I see my cousin's ghost/Seeking out Romeo'. Tybalt's death was violent and could suggest his spirit would not be at peace. The strong religious beliefs of both Juliet and Shakespeare's contemporary audience would make this a very real fear.

Italian society – Now you try! (page 27)
Capulet shows his power when he is enraged by Juliet's refusal to marry Paris. His attitude towards Juliet changes rapidly when he proclaims he will 'give you to my friend'. Shakespeare shows us how women were viewed in Veronese society at the time: Juliet is referred to here as a possession that can be disposed of at her father's will.

Quick revision – Quick quiz (page 29)
1. They were all male 2. Romeo; Juliet 3. Italy 4. Friar Lawrence; Romeo; Juliet 5. The heads of wealthy families 6. A society which is led by powerful males 7. To extend the wealth, power and status of the Capulet family and provide a secure future for Juliet 8. Mercutio; Tybalt 9. The Capulet orchard 10. Friar Lawrence

Quick revision – Power paragraphs (page 29)
- The Capulet crypt is an important setting in the play as it is the place to which Juliet must be taken when she fakes her own death. The fear of the crypt and what may be there causes Juliet distress and anxiety as she is about to take the potion. She imagines, 'loathsome smells' and 'shrieks like mandrakes' that would come from 'all my buried ancestors'.
- These imaginings of Juliet are, however, nowhere near as terrifying as the reality Juliet faces when she wakes in the tomb to find that Romeo has met 'his timeless end'. The vault becomes the place where the lovers are tragically reunited and where their families are reunited through their grief.

CHARACTERS

Romeo (Acts I and II) – Now you try! (page 31)
However, we see a serious side to Romeo when he meets with the Nurse. Here we see how he is determined in his love and promises that Juliet 'shall at Friar Lawrence's cell/Be shriv'd and married'. This convinces the audience that Romeo isn't just lovesick and fickle, but capable of making a commitment and genuine in his feelings.

Romeo (Acts III–V) – Now you try! (page 33)
Romeo can also be seen to be loving and supportive when he takes his leave of Juliet after their wedding night. Despite her sense of foreboding he aims to convince her that 'all these woes shall serve/For sweet discourses in our times to come.' This is a bittersweet moment however, as the audience already know from the Prologue that the lovers will not have those times.

Juliet (Acts I and II) – Now you try! (page 35)
Shakespeare shows us how Juliet can behave in a way that is hasty and impatient. She anxiously awaits news from the Nurse, asking her, 'What says he of our marriage, what of that?' This shows that Juliet is capable of acting on impulse and without thinking carefully about the consequences of marrying Romeo without her parents' knowledge.

Juliet (Acts III–V) – Now you try! (page 37)
Shakespeare presents Juliet as capable of feeling strong passions and she is defiant when she hears the news of the marriage to Paris. She is bold in exclaiming, 'He shall not make me there a joyful bride', showing her more headstrong side. However, her reaction here is justified in that Juliet is already married to Romeo. The audience are aware of why she is so defiant, though her parents are not, creating dramatic tension in the scene.

Mercutio and Tybalt – Now you try! (page 39)
In this way, Mercutio could be seen as having some similarities with Tybalt as he too is hot headed and is seen to provoke acts of violence in the play. In the opening of the play, Tybalt dismisses Benvolio's request for peace by claiming, 'I hate the word.' He is quick to reach for his sword in any encounter with the Montagues.

ANSWERS

Lord and Lady Capulet – Now you try! (page 41)
In Act III, Lady Capulet speaks to Juliet in a way that is surprising in the blunt way she introduces the topic of marriage. She instructs her to 'think of marriage now' and seems far more keen than Lord Capulet at this point to secure her daughter's marriage to Paris.

The Nurse and Friar Lawrence – Now you try! (page 43)
Similarly, one of the Friar's functions in the play is to advise the two young lovers. However, as events become more fraught, the Friar's advice and plans become more dangerous, particularly when he offers Juliet 'a kind of hope/Which craves as desperate an execution/As that is desperate which we would prevent'. Like many of the other characters, the Friar is capable of unwise decision-making and rash actions.

Benvolio and Paris – Now you try! (page 45)
Similarly, Paris is presented as a sensitive character, who behaves with propriety throughout. His use of the term 'Sweet flower' suggests he has genuine affection for Juliet which we see most closely when he visits the vault after her supposed death.

Quick revision – Timeline (page 46)
Romeo is sad and lovesick: E; Romeo becomes a risk taker as he falls deeply in love: C; Romeo shows he can be angry and seek revenge: A; Romeo acts hastily and with violence: B; Romeo shows deep regret and distress: D

Quick revision – Quick quiz (pages 46–7)
1. Romeo is infatuated with her at the start of the play 2. Capulet to introduce Paris to his daughter 3. Paris 4. The Nurse 5. Tybalt 6. Mercutio 7. The Nurse 8. Friar Lawrence 9. Peter 10. Tybalt 11. Juliet 12. Mercutio 13. Lady Capulet 14. The Nurse 15. Friar Lawrence 16. Juliet 17. Paris 18. Lord Capulet 19. The Nurse 20. The apothecary

Quick revision – Power paragraphs (page 47)
1. Benvolio is presented from the start of the play as calm and rational and the one who tries to prevent any further violence from erupting on the streets of Verona through his pleas to 'Put up your swords'. By contrast, Mercutio is more spontaneous and easily provoked. He has a keen sense of family pride and is quick to respond to Tybalt's violent threats: 'Tybalt, you rat-catcher, will you walk?' As a result of this Mercutio loses his life, whilst Benvolio loses his closest friends.
2. Shakespeare shows Paris to be respectful and honourable. He visits the Capulet family following the death of Tybalt and pays his respects asking Lady Capulet to merely 'commend me to your daughter'. He behaves with propriety and follows polite conventions. In this way he is shown to be a contrast to Romeo, whose hasty and passionate actions have jeopardised his relationship with Juliet.

Quick revision – Exam practice (page 47)
- In this extract Capulet's character changes swiftly from the seemingly gentle and caring father we saw in Act I. Here his authority and decision-making are challenged by Juliet's refusal of the marriage and at first he cannot believe what he is hearing, 'Soft, take me with you, take me with you, wife.' This disbelief turns to rage and we can see how violently Capulet can behave when provoked.
- Capulet berates, insults and threatens Juliet, disregarding any pleas from the Nurse or Lady Capulet to calm down. It would seem that Capulet is both angered and insulted that Juliet would turn down the 'gentleman of noble parentage' he has arranged for her to marry. His pride and honour are at stake and he exerts his power as head of the household by referring to Juliet as a possession when he states he will 'give you to my friend'.

THEMES

Love – Now you try! (page 49)
Shakespeare also shows us that love can be dangerous when Romeo and Juliet are warned by the Friar that, 'These violent delights have violent ends', which becomes a chilling prediction of the events to come later in the play. The Friar advises the lovers to 'love moderately' – the speed and passion of their immediate attraction and swift marriage is in direct contrast to this warning, which comes too late as they are about to take their vows.

Fate and free will – Now you try! (page 51)
Shakespeare shows Romeo to believe that fate is shaping his future when he is wary of attending the Capulet feast. He has a sense of foreboding and suspects that 'some consequence yet hanging in the stars/Shall bitterly begin his fearful date/with this night's revels.' Despite his superstitious nature, he disregards this feeling and attends the feast, thereby creating the opportunity for that 'consequence' to happen.

Family and marriage – Now you try! (page 53)
Shakespeare shows us a different attitude towards marriage when Capulet is angry with Juliet for refusing Paris. He seems to consider marriage as a transaction or business deal that he has worked on, 'Day, night, work, play', which is a direct contrast to the fast, spontaneous immediate attraction the lovers experience at the feast.

Conflict and honour – Now you try! (page 55)
Another character for whom honour is important is Tybalt. However, he sees honour as being something that can be defended only by violence and seems to behave more dishonourably as a result. He displays this misguided sense of family honour when he tells Benvolio that he 'hates hell, all Montagues, and thee'. He does not consider that his actions may be dishonourable or may bring punishment to the family from the Prince.

85

ANSWERS

Quick revision – Quick quiz (pages 56–7)
1. Romeo and Juliet 2. Juliet 3. Romeo 4. Capulet 5. Lady Montague 6. Montague 7. Tybalt 8. The Nurse 9. Mercutio 10. Benvolio 11. The Nurse 12. Lady Capulet 13. Romeo 14. Juliet 15. Death 16. Lady Capulet 17. Friar Lawrence 18. Friar Lawrence's cell 19. Lady Montague 20. We hear of three brawls in Act I and then one more in Act III – so a total of four.

Quick revision – Power paragraphs (page 57)
1. Whilst Lord Capulet is presented as a caring father, Lady Capulet seems somewhat cold and distant from Juliet from the start. Indeed, we learn that most of Juliet's upbringing was done by the Nurse. This suggests that Juliet's parents do not know her as well as they think and are unaware of her true nature, which, when she defies their wishes, leads them to consider her as, 'unworthy' of the marriage they have arranged for her.
2. Romeo and Juliet defy the social conventions of the time by choosing each other and marrying in secret without the consent of either set of parents. In this way they place themselves in danger as a result of the 'ancient grudge' that stands between their families, which often erupts into violence.

Quick revision – Exam practice (page 57)
- Mercutio is astounded that Romeo has not risen to the challenge that Tybalt has made to him and cannot understand his 'vile submission'. At this point in the play the Montagues are totally unaware of Romeo's marriage and the reasons why Romeo chooses to try to keep the peace.
- Mercutio's haste in stepping in to take Tybalt's challenge leads to his death as Romeo tries in vain to separate them. This death acts as a catalyst because Romeo swiftly avenges the death of his close friend, who 'got his mortal hurt/In my behalf'. He considers too late the 'consequence', which earlier in the play gave him such a feeling of foreboding.

LANGUAGE

Imagery and symbolism – Now you try! (page 59)
Shakespeare presents the Friar as a knowledgeable man when collecting 'baleful weeds and precious-juiced flowers' outside his cell. This helps us to see that the Friar has abilities in medicine and potions and it hints at events later in the play when these natural plants are used to create Juliet's unnatural 'death'.

Dramatic techniques – Now you try! (page 61)
Shakespeare uses foreshadowing when Juliet imagines Romeo 'As one dead in the bottom of a tomb'. This is a grim precursor to the next time Juliet sees Romeo, when he is indeed dead beside her in the Capulet's vault.

EXAM PRACTICE

Planning your character response – Now you try! (page 67)
- Paragraph 1: Friar Lawrence knows Romeo well, and has knowledge of his previous anxieties about love, e.g. he mentions Rosaline here. He understands how emotional and sensitive Romeo can be. We see this later in the play when he advises and calms Romeo after news of his banishment.
- Paragraph 2: The Friar warns Romeo about how quickly he has changed his mind about Rosaline, 'art thou chang'd'. This reminds us of Capulet's feast when Romeo seems to be attracted to Juliet (and vice versa) and falls in love with her almost immediately.
- Paragraph 3: The Friar tries to teach Romeo the difference between 'doting' and 'loving' (the meaning of genuine feelings). This scene comes after the balcony scene when Romeo and Juliet pledge their love and decide to marry. It's as if the advice is already too late.
- Paragraph 4: The Friar warns Romeo about his desire for 'haste'; he should slow down and think 'Wisely and slow'. Good advice but the Friar marries the lovers quickly and does not follow his own advice.
- Paragraph 5: Friar Lawrence can see positives in the relationship – the marriage may help to heal the feud ('rancour' to 'pure love'). But is he thinking of the consequences? At the end of the play when he cannot fulfil his promise to reunite the lovers, he abandons Juliet.

Grade 5 sample answer – Check the skills (page 69)
Points: There are some clear points about Juliet wanting to feel secure and sure of Romeo. Also it shows she is serious about the relationship and wants to know Romeo is equally serious.
Context: There are some hints about the way girls in wealthy households were expected to behave at the time.
Interpretations: The paragraphs suggest that Juliet has loyal, open and honest qualities but there is a contradiction: she is planning to keep her love for Romeo a secret.

Grade 5 sample answer – Now you try! (page 69)
Though Romeo and Juliet are honest and open with each other in the extract, Juliet is worried that Romeo may perceive her to be immodest and too quick to agree to a relationship with him. She gently and humorously suggests she could 'frown and be perverse' – perhaps behaving like Rosaline. She implies that perhaps she should be more coy and hold back her feelings. However, this is somewhat ironic as Juliet is able to mask her true feelings and be a convincing actress when she convinces the Nurse she has gone 'to make confession' after angering Capulet later in the play.

ANSWERS

Grade 7+ sample answer - Check the skills (page 71)
Fluent ideas: Paragraph four has a link from the extract to the rest of the play with the comment on irony. The opening of paragraph five leads from this and embeds a good choice of quotation.
Language and techniques: The two paragraphs have comments about metaphor, irony and contrast; they are written in a subtle and fluent way.
Deeper insight: Both paragraphs show a good knowledge of the whole play, for example linking Tybalt's death and the night in the tomb to Juliet's loyalty.

Grade 7+ sample answer - Now you try! (page 71)
AO1
- The Friar knows Romeo and his situation well, as trusted adviser and confidante.
- Shocked and surprised at Romeo's change of heart, link to earlier in the play when lovesick for Rosaline.
- Advises Romeo against hasty action, contradicted by his marrying the couple later in the Act.
- Thinks there may be positives from this change of heart though he does not think of the full implications of the marriage on the families later in the play.

AO2
- Use of exclamations for his shock and surprise, 'Holy Saint Francis!'
- Use of questioning, 'And art thou chang'd?'
- Use of oppositions 'rancour'/'pure love' and 'haste'/'slow' to consider positives and negatives of the situation.

AO3
- Shakespeare highlights a religious context and the value placed on the Friar/religious faith.
- Romeo turns to the Friar and not his parents for advice, giving clue about the parent–child relationship.
- Shakespeare gives us social and moral messages about love and marriage and how it was perceived at the time.

Planning your theme response - Now you try! (page 75)
Paragraph 1: Juliet is anxious for night and Romeo to arrive. The secrecy of young love is emphasised by 'runaways' eyes', contrasting with a later scene when Romeo is leaving and Nurse/her mother interrupts them.
Paragraph 2: Shakespeare emphasises Juliet's youth and innocence: 'stainless maidenhoods', 'modesty', reminders us of the feast when Romeo kissed her hand.
Paragraph 3: Despite their innocence there are references to sexual attraction: 'amorous rites', 'not yet enjoy'd'. Juliet is passionately awaiting her wedding night, linking with later in the play when she is determined not to marry Paris and stay faithful to 'my Romeo'.
Paragraph 4: Night is a theme in the extract, comparing their love to night time and the stars/moon. Shakespeare presents young love as 'gentle' like the stars, linking with the scene in the orchard where Romeo uses images of the moon/stars.

Paragraph 5: Shakespeare still emphasises the haste/speed of the relationship: 'Give me my Romeo', 'Leap to these arms'. Friar Lawrence warns: 'Wisely and slow'.

Grade 5 sample answer - Check the skills (page 77)
Points: These paragraphs show how the couple married out of free choice with serious consequences. One of these is the second, arranged marriage to Paris, which Juliet was not expecting.
Context: There are some references to fate and comments about the consequences of marrying in secret and without permission at that time.
Interpretation: The student has thought about how fate or fortune seems to have turned on the couple; how they seem to have been victims of bad luck, as if their choices are to blame for this.

Grade 5 sample answer - Now you try! (page 77)
Shakespeare has used foreshadowing extensively in the play and this creates the effect of the lovers' future being almost written in the stars. Most grim here is when Juliet compares Romeo climbing down from her room, 'As one dead in the bottom of a tomb'. This poignant parting of the young lovers is both heart-wrenching and terrifying when we realise that the next time they meet will be at the Capulet vault. Shakespeare here sows seeds of the tragedy to come, hinting that the future will involve 'death's pale flag' and will not be the happy one presented by Romeo.

Grade 7+ sample answer - Check the skills (page 79)
Fluent ideas: The paragraphs show how Romeo and Juliet share the blame for their actions. They also show a good knowledge of the different parts of the play that link to the themes of fate and free will.
Context: Paragraph four links the theme of free will to how people were expected to behave at the time.
Deeper insight: The student discusses Romeo and Juliet's view of fate against their own choices and behaviour. Paragraph five looks at dramatic irony, and links this to the end of the play.

Grade 7+ sample answer - Now you try! (page 79)
AO1
- Juliet's enthusiasm for her wedding night ahead.
- The secrecy of their relationship.
- The youth and innocence of both Romeo and Juliet.
- The idea of the night and secrecy.
- The idea of hastiness and speed perhaps linked to thoughtless actions and risk.

AO2
- Numerous references to darkness and hiding/secrecy; personification of the night.
- Use of contrast, e.g. images of innocence contrasted with references to sexual love.
- Imagery connected to the stars.
- Use of imperatives.

AO3
- Links to the conventions of marriage at the time.
- Juliet as young girl in patriarchal society.
- Consequences of secret marriage without parental permission.

Practice questions (pages 80-1)

Question 6
AO1
- In this extract, Shakespeare shows how little Lady Capulet knows her own daughter or appreciates her feelings.
- We see Juliet's panic and distress at this possible second marriage.
- We see how Lady Capulet leaves Juliet to deal with the wrath of her father and does not support her.
- The play as a whole reveals that the Nurse has brought up Juliet and it seems that Juliet and her mother are not close.
- This is reinforced through the fact that Juliet cannot confide in her mother or tell her the truth about Romeo – turning instead to the Nurse. She asks her mother to leave her alone the night before the wedding to Paris.
- Only when Juliet is found 'dead' on the morning of her wedding does Lady Capulet show real emotion for her loss.

AO2
- In this extract, the phrase 'joyful bride' is ironic given that Juliet has just spent her wedding night with Romeo.
- Juliet uses a defiant tone: 'I will not marry …'.
- The use of the exclamation reveals her shock and surprise at the news and suggests her sense of panic.
- In the play as a whole, Juliet's mother is often brisk and business-like in her tone with Juliet: 'How stands your disposition to be married?'
- Juliet refers to her mother as 'madam' and her nurse as 'gentle Nurse' on the night she takes the potion.

AO3
- The extract reveals the reality of arranged marriages for young girls from wealthy families.
- It shows the gender divide in that Lady Capulet appears almost frightened to give the news to Capulet and leaves this task to Juliet herself.
- We learn that Juliet's mother was married to Capulet young and this reinforces the social conventions of the time.
- The character of the Nurse gives insight into how the children of the wealthy are brought up.

Question 7
AO1
- Family power operates in this extract via the way Capulet organises Juliet's marriage.
- Capulet makes all of the decisions including the day of the wedding.
- He sends his wife to inform Juliet and we also see him commanding the servants, reinforcing his position as head of the household.
- The whole play centres around the actions of two powerful families and we note they are led by powerful men – as is Verona itself.
- We witness the rivalry between the families through the two outbreaks of violence between the young men of the two households.
- We see the consequences of the lovers going against their powerful families.

AO2
- Capulet uses the verb 'ruled' to suggest that Juliet will willingly comply with his plans.
- Shakespeare uses minor sentences and questions to increase the pace and this seems to show Capulet's haste in arranging something so significant for his only daughter.
- He uses imperatives, 'Go you', 'Prepare her, wife', to issue commands to his wife.
- In other parts of the play, Shakespeare uses the speech and proclamation of the Prince to reinforce the impact of the hierarchy of power in Verona. This occurs both in the opening and at the play's conclusion.
- Shakespeare uses references to the family names of Montague and Capulet throughout the play to reinforce the divisions between them.
- Shakespeare uses contrast between the quiet scenes of love and the much more violent scenes where family honour is at stake.

AO3
- We see a patriarchal society in which the father as head of the household makes all of the decisions.
- Additionally, we see a society where women are forced to be subordinate to men and take a secondary role.
- Throughout the play there is a strict social hierarchy of power with the Prince at the top.
- We witness the impact of wealthy families and the consequences of their feuds and disagreements on one of the city-states of Italy at this time.